PEANUTS JUBILEE

By Charles M. Schulz

Penguin Books

To Jim Freeman, who opened the first package

Penguin Books Ltd, Harmondsworth, Middlesex, England
Penguin Books, 625 Madison Avenue, New York, New York 10022, U.S.A.
Penguin Books Australia Ltd, Ringwood, Victoria, Australia
Penguin Books Canada Ltd, 41 Steelcase Road West, Markham,
Ontario, Canada
Penguin Books (N.Z.) Ltd, 182-190 Wairau Road, Auckland 10, New Zealand

First published in the U.S.A 1975
Published in Great Britain byAllen Lane 1976
Published in Penguin Books 1976

Copyright © United Feature Syndicate, Inc., 1975

Made and printed in the U.S.A.

CONTENTS

PEANUTS JUBILEE

1 And so, 25 years have gone by. At one strip per day, that comes to almost 10,000 comic strips. Actually, this is not so much when you consider the longevity of many other comic features. Employees receive wristwatches if they have put in this much time with a company, but a comic-strip artist just keeps on drawing. (Somehow a comic-strip artist is never regarded as an employee.) I have been asked many times if I ever dreamed that Peanuts would become as successful as it is, and I think I always surprise people when I say, "Well, frankly, I guess I did expect it, because, after all, it was something I had planned for since I was six years old." Obviously I did not know that Snoopy was going to go to the moon, and I did not know that the phrase "happiness is a warm puppy" would prompt hundreds of other such definitions, and I did not know that the term "security blanket" would become part of the American language; but I did have the hope that I would be able to contribute something to a profession that I can say now I have loved all my life.

It is important to me, when I am discussing comic strips, to make certain that everyone knows that I do not regard what I am doing as Great Art. I am certainly not ashamed of the work I do, nor do I apologize for being involved in a field that is generally regarded as occupying a very low rung on the entertainment ladder. I am all too aware of the fact that when a reviewer for a sophisticated journal wishes to downgrade the latest Broadway play, one of the worst things he can say about it is that it has a comic-strip plot. This is also true for movie reviewers, but I tend to believe that movies, as a whole, really do not rank that much higher than comic strips as an art form. The comic strip can be an extremely creative form of endeavor. On its highest level, we find a wonderful combination of writing and drawing, generally done by one man sitting at a drawing board in a room all by himself, much the same as a composer sitting at a piano, or a writer crouched over his typewriter. But there are several factors that work against comic strips, preventing them from becoming a true art form in the mind of the public. In the first place, they are reproduced with the express purpose of helping publishers sell their publications. The paper on which they appear is not of the best quality, so the reproductions lose much of the beauty of the originals. The artist is also forced to serve many masters—he must please the syndicate editor, as well as the countless editors who purchase his comic strip. The strip is not always exhibited in the best place, but is forced to compete on the same page with other strips that may be printed larger or enjoy a better position. And there are always annoying things like copyright stickers, which can break up the pleasing design of a panel, or the intrusion of titles into first panels in order to save space. The true artist, working on his canvas, does not have to put up with such desecrations.

There is a trend these days to try to prove that comic strips are true art by exhibiting them in galleries, either for people simply to enjoy viewing, or for customers to purchase. It seems to me that although this is a laudable effort, it is begging the question, because how we distinguish something doesn't matter nearly as much as the purpose it serves. The comic strip serves its purpose in an admirable way, for there is no medium that can compete with it for readership or for longevity. There are numerous comic strips that have been enjoyed by as many as 60 million readers a day, for a period of fifty years. Having a large audience does not, of course, prove that something is necessarily good, and I subscribe to the theory that only a creation that speaks to succeeding generations can truly be labeled art. Unfortunately, very few comic strips seem to do this.

In my earliest recollections of drawing I seem to be at a small blackboard with a paper roller at the top on which are printed the ABC's. It was from this roller that I was able to learn the alphabet before I began kindergarten, and I know that I drew constantly on the blackboard and had it for many years.

It may have been on the first day at kindergarten, or at least during the first week, when the teacher handed out big crayons and huge sheets of white wrapping paper and told us to lie on the floor and draw something. Several of my mother's relatives had recently moved from the Twin Cities to Needles, California, and I had heard my mother reading a letter from one of them telling of the sandstorms in Needles and also describing the tall palm trees. So when the teacher told us to draw whatever came to our minds, being familiar with the Minnesota snowstorms I drew a man shoveling snow, but then added a palm tree to the background.

I recall being somewhat puzzled when I was drawing the snow shovel because I was not quite sure how to put it in proper perspective. I knew that drawing the shovel square was not right, but I didn't know how to solve the problem. At any rate, it didn't seem to bother the teacher. She came around during the project, looked down at my drawing and said, "Someday, Charles, you're going to be an artist."

I never knew what family problems caused us to make the move, but in 1930, when I was six years old, my mother and father and I drove from St. Paul to Needles in a 1928 Ford. I believe the trip took us almost two weeks. We remained in Needles for almost a year and I suppose there were some happy times, but I think my dad was disillusioned with what he saw. He had intended to continue northwest and settle in Sacramento, but somehow he never made the final move.

After a year, we moved back to St. Paul and he repurchased his barbershop. I have memories of the trip to Needles, but I don't remember a single thing about the return trip to St. Paul. We settled in a neighborhood about two blocks from

The resemblance to Charlie Brown is quite apparent, although he has never had as much to laugh about. I was given the nickname of Sparky at the age of two days, after Barney Google's horse, Sparkplug. "Barney Google" was at the height of its fame at that time.

my dad's barbershop and most of my playtime life revolved around the yard of the grade school across the street from our apartment. In the wintertime we played in the deep snow, and in the summertime we either played baseball in the schoolyard or used its sandy wastes as the Sahara Desert when inspired by seeing movies such as *The Lost Patrol* with Victor McLaglen.

I was drawing cartoons during these years but created very few original characters. Most of the time I copied Buck Rogers or Walt Disney figures, or some of the characters in "Tim Tyler's Luck." I was fascinated by the animals in this feature.

Early influences on my work were many. I continued to be a great fan of all of the Disney characters when I was in grade school, and I also enjoyed Popeye and Wimpy very much. I used to decorate my loose-leaf binders with drawings of Mickey Mouse, The Three Little Pigs, and Popeye, and whenever friends in class would see these cartoons, I would be asked to draw them on their notebooks as well. I used to buy every Big Little Book and comic magazine that came out and study all of the various cartoonists' techniques. When I reached high school age, the work of Milt Caniff and Al Capp influenced me considerably, as well as that of some of the earlier cartoonists such as Clare Briggs ("When a Fella Needs a Friend"). I also thought there was no one who drew funnier and more warmhearted cartoons than J. R. Williams.

11

But the man who influenced me most was Roy Crane with his drawings of Wash Tubbs and Captain Easy. His rollicking style laid the groundwork for many cartoonists who followed him. A book collection of "Krazy Kat" was published sometime in the late 1940s, which did much to inspire me to create a feature that went beyond the mere actions of ordinary children. After World War II, I began to study the "Krazy Kat" strip for the first time, for during my younger years I never had the opportunity to see a newspaper that carried it.

Also in my high school years, I became a Sherlock Holmes fanatic and used to buy scrapbooks at the local five-and-dime and fill them with Sherlock Holmes stories in comic-book form. A friend of mine named Shermy was one of my faithful readers, and when I started Peanuts I used his name for one of the original characters.

My scholastic career got off to a good start when I was very young. I received a special diploma in the second grade for being the outstanding boy student, and in the third and fifth grades I was moved ahead so suddenly that I was the smallest kid in the class. Somehow, I survived the early years of grade school, but when I entered junior high school, I failed everything in sight. High school proved not much better. There was no doubt that I was absolutely the worst physics student in the history of St. Paul Central High School. It was not until I became a senior that I earned any respectable grades at all.

I have often felt that some semblance of maturity began to arrive at last. I saved that final report card because it was the only one that seemed to justify those long years of agony.

While I was a senior, my very fine teacher of illustration, Miss Minette Paro, invited me to draw a series of cartoons about some of the activities around school for our senior annual. I was delighted to do this and set about it quickly, and promptly presented the drawings to Miss Paro. She seemed pleased with them, and I looked forward to the publishing of our yearbook, where I expected finally to see my cartoons on the printed page. The last day of school arrived and I thumbed anxiously through the annual, but found none of my drawings. To this day, I do not know why they were rejected. I have enjoyed a certain revenge, however, for ever since Peanuts was created I have received a steady stream of requests from high schools around the country to use the characters in their yearbooks. Eventually I accumulated a stack tall enough to reach the ceiling.

I think it is important for adults to consider what they were doing and what their attitudes were when they were the age their own children are now. There is no other real way of understanding the problems of children.

Charlie Brown's father is a barber, which is autobiographical, for our family's life revolved around the long hours my dad spent in his barbershop. He loved his work very much.

HIGH SCHOOL

MONTHLY REPORT

Semester Ending _____June_____ 19 40

Name _Schulz, Charles_

Enrollment Room _315_

Subjects	Room	1	2	3	4	Ex.	Av.	Cred-its
1 Econ.	315	A	A	B	B		85	
2 M. 3	319	a	a+	a	a		94	
3 St.	A							
4 St.	301							
5 Com. Law	217	B		H	A		86	
6 M.	319	a	a	a	a		93	
7								
8								
Days Absent			1	1				
Times Tardy				1				

95 to 100 Excellent, AA.   90 to 94, Very Good, A.
85 to 89 Good, B.   80 to 84 Fair, C.
75 to 79 Passing, D.   Below 75 Failure, E.

SIGNATURE OF PARENT OR GUARDIAN

1st Mo. _Mrs. Carl Schulz_
2nd Mo. _Mrs. Carl Schulz_
3rd Mo. _Mrs. Carl Schulz_
4th Mo. _____

This report card is printed to show my own children that I was not as dumb as everyone has said I was. It is quite apparent, however, that I had an easy schedule during the last half semester. It was probably the only few months when I ever enjoyed school.

(Overleaf) *In high school we had our choice of music, art, illustration, or some shop classes. I was incapable of sawing a piece of wood straight or of hammering a nail without splitting the grain, and I hated music because of the embarrassment of being forced to sing. Art classes bored me with such projects as making linoleum cuts or doing watercolors of flowers. What I really wanted to do was draw. Fortunately, Miss Paro's class in illustration seemed to be the answer. One day she told us to draw anything we could think of in groups of three. Somehow, this was to stimulate our imaginations. I swung into the project with great enthusiasm. I filled the eleven-by-fourteen-inch sheet of paper with all sorts of little cartoons, and it is interesting today to look back at that project and to see how I was affected by the times and by what was going on in my life. The telephones were the old-fashioned type. I drew three little Hitlers, three Wheaties cereal boxes, three barber poles—because of my father—and various sports equipment. All in all, it was a thoroughly enjoyable project, and I remember Miss Paro asking me to stand and read off a list of the objects I had drawn, and my feeling of triumph that my list was much longer than that of anyone else in the class. I handed in the paper proudly. Twenty-five years later, I received a rather thick envelope in the mail, and when I opened it I could not believe my eyes. There was the sheet of paper on which I had drawn those very cartoons in groups of three. A little note from Miss Paro explained that she frequently saved some of the work of her students, and she thought I might be interested in having it. Since then she and I have kept up a slight correspondence, and it has always been a joy to hear from her.*

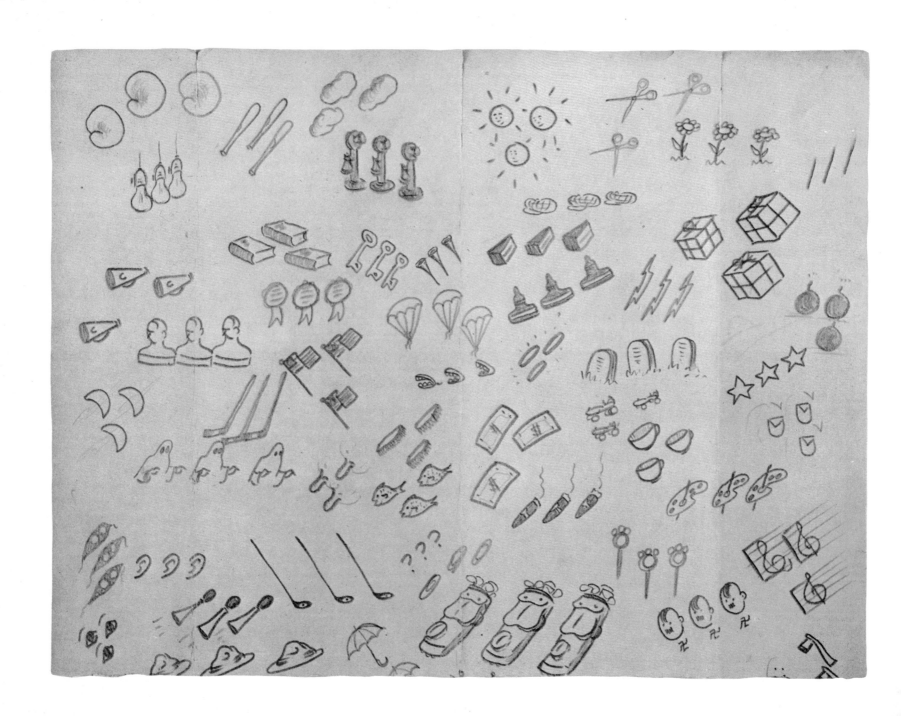

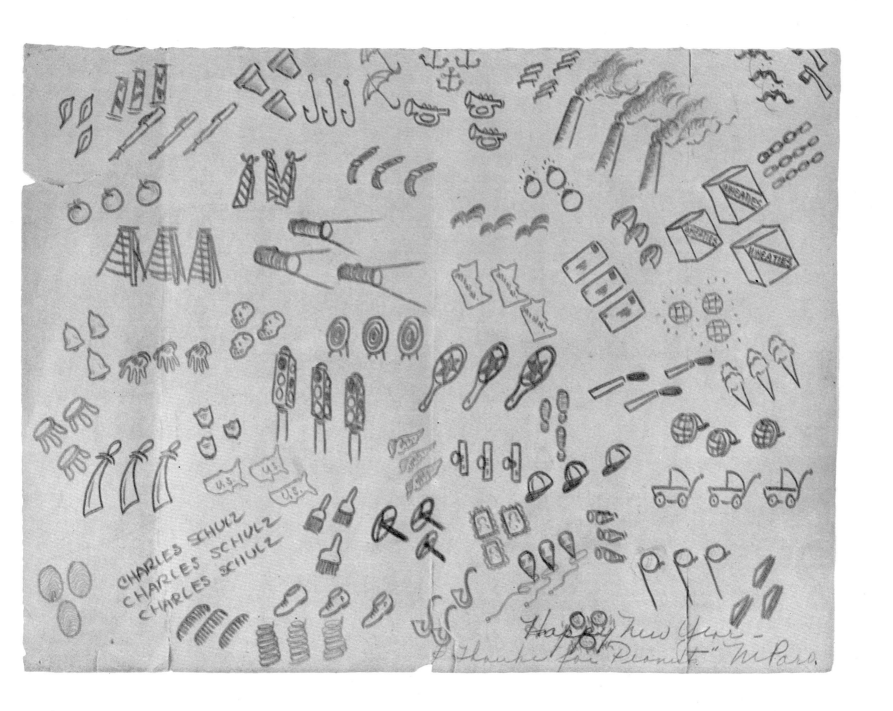

CHARLES SCHULZ
CHARLES SCHULZ
CHARLES SCHULZ

I recall him telling me once that he really enjoyed getting up in the morning and going off to work. He was always in the barbershop by 8:00 in the morning, and during the 1930s he always worked until at least 6:30, and on Friday and Saturday nights, many times, until 8:00 or 9:00. He had one day off each week, Sunday, and his favorite sport was fishing. Occasionally, he would take my mother and me to a night baseball game or a hockey game, but fishing was always his main interest. It must have been disappointing to have a son who preferred golf.

Frequently in the evenings I went to the barbershop to wait for him to finish work and then walk home with him. He loved to read the comic strips, and we discussed them together and worried about what was going to happen next to certain of the characters. On Saturday evening, I would run up to the local drugstore at 9:00 when the Sunday pages were delivered and buy the two Minneapolis papers. The next morning, the two St. Paul papers would be delivered, so we had four comic sections to read. Several years later, when I became a delivery boy for one of the local printing firms, I used to pass the windows of the St. Paul *Pioneer Press* and look in where I could see the huge presses and the Sunday funnies tumbling down across the rollers. I wondered if I would ever see my own comics on those presses.

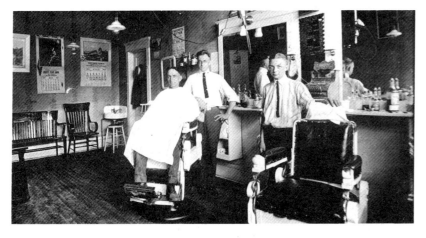 

I was eighteen when this family picture was taken. A much earlier picture, taken I believe in 1921, shows my dad's barbershop; my Uncle Monroe stands behind the empty chair. The shop hadn't changed much by the time I was growing up—dad had added another chair at the front, which was the one he worked at most of the time. The other snapshots is of my mother sitting beside the 1934 Ford I have mentioned (and have sometimes referred to in the strip).

My mother also encouraged me in my drawing but, sadly, never lived to see any of my work published. She died a long, lingering death from cancer, when I was twenty, and it was a loss from which I sometimes believe I never recovered. Today it is a source of astonishment to me that I am older than she was when she died, and realizing this saddens me even more.

When I was thirteen, we were given a black-and-white dog who turned out to be the forerunner of Snoopy. He was a mixed breed and slightly larger than the beagle Snoopy is supposed to be. He probably had a little pointer in him and some other kind of hound, but he was a wild creature; I don't believe he was ever completely tamed. He had a "vocabulary" of understanding of approximately fifty words, and he loved to ride in the car. He waited all day for my dad to come home from the barbershop, and on Saturday evenings, just before 9:00, he always put his paws on my dad's chair to let him know it was time to get in the car and make the short drive up to the store to buy those newspapers. When I decided to put a dog in Peanuts, I used the general appearance of Spike, with similar markings. I had decided that the dog in the strip was to be named Sniffy, until one day, just before the strip was actually to be published, I was walking past a newsstand and glanced down at the rows of comic magazines. There I saw one about a dog named Sniffy, so I had to go back to my room and think of another name. Fortunately, before I even

got home, I recalled my mother once saying that if we ever had another dog, we should name him Snoopy.

Not long ago I was looking through *The Art of Walt Disney*, a beautiful book, and there was a list of names that had been considered for The Seven Dwarfs. Lo and behold, one of the names that had been considered, but turned down, was Snoopy.

In my childhood, sports played a reasonably strong role, although they were strictly the sandlot variety. There was no organized Little League for us, even though we were all quite fanatical about baseball. Living in Minnesota restricted much of our sports activity, for the warmer seasons were short and clearly defined. Spring meant the coming of the marble season, and I loved playing marbles. When the baseball season came, we organized our own team and challenged those of other neighborhoods. We rarely had good fields for our games, and it was always our dream to play on a smooth infield and actually have a backstop behind the catcher so we wouldn't have to chase the foul balls. All too often, we would have to lift a manhole cover and lower someone to retrieve a baseball that had rolled along the curb and down into the sewer. We played a little tackle football, but more often touch football, as it was clearly less rough and did not have to be played on soft ground. In Minnesota, almost everyone knows how to skate, but I didn't actually learn on a real skating rink. Every

Spike was a mixed breed, probably part pointer. The similarity to Snoopy is at least in the markings. Spike would eat almost anything in sight. One day I was playing with a paddle and ball in the backyard and the rubberband broke, and Spike chased down the ball, grabbed it, and swallowed it. That night, after eating too much spaghetti, he threw it back up. Not long afterward, I made this drawing of Spike and sent it in to Ripley's Believe It or Not. *It was my first published drawing.*

sidewalk in front of every school had a sheet of ice at least ten feet long worn smooth from the kids sliding on it. It was on such a patch of ice, no longer than ten feet or wider than three feet, that I learned to skate. To play hockey on a real rink was a hopeless dream. Our hockey was usually played on a very tiny rink in one of our backyards, or in the street where we simply ran around with shoes rather than skates. The goals were two large clumps of snow, which were easily destroyed by inconsiderate drivers. I had always wanted to play golf, and had seen a series of Bobby Jones movie shorts when I was nine years old. There was no one to show me the game, and it was not until I was fifteen that I had a chance to try it. Immediately I fell totally in love with golf. I could think of almost nothing else for the next few years. I still wanted to be a cartoonist, but I also dreamed of becoming a great amateur golfer. Unfortunately, I never won anything except the caddy championship of Highland Park.

There are certain seasons in our lives that each of us can recall, and there are others that disappear from our memories like the melting snow. When I was fourteen, I had a summer that I shall always remember. We had organized our own neighborhood baseball team, but we never played on a strict schedule, for we didn't know when we could find another team to play. I lived about a block from a grade school called Maddocks in St. Paul where there was a rather large crushed-rock playground, which did have two baseball backstops, but no fences. A hard-hit ground ball could elude the second baseman or shortstop and very easily roll into the outfield so fast that none of the outfielders would be able to stop it, and it would be quite possible for a fast runner to beat it out for a home run. This field also could make sliding into second base reasonably painful if you were not careful. Fortunately, it was smooth enough so ground balls hit to the infielders did not take too many bad bounces.

A man named Harry (I never knew his last name) was the playground director that summer. He saw our interest in playing baseball and came up with the idea that we should organize four teams and have a summer league. This was the most exciting news that had come to any of us in a long time. There were two games each Tuesday and Thursday and I could hardly wait for them to begin. One game was to start at 9:00 between two of the teams, and the other game was to start at 10:30 between the other two teams. I was always at the field by 7:30 with all of my equipment, waiting for something to happen. Our team came in first place that year, probably because we practiced more than the other teams, and one day I actually pitched a no-hit, no-run game. It was a great summer and I wish that there were some way I could let that man, whom we knew only as Harry, know how much I appreciated it.

We knew little about Harry because boys that age are never quite that interested in people older than they. At my mother's suggestion, all the boys on our team chipped in and bought him a cake one day to demonstrate our appreciation for what he had done for us. He was a gentle man, probably not more than twenty-three or twenty-four, and I doubt if he was married. This was probably only a temporary job for him during times when it was difficult to find work, but he did his job well and he gave all of us a happy summer.

I have always tried to dig beneath the surface in my sports cartoons by drawing upon an intimate knowledge of the games. The challenges to be faced in sports work marvelously as a caricature of the challenges that we face in the more serious aspects of our lives. Anytime I experienced a crushing defeat in bowling, or had a bad night at bridge, or failed to qualify in the opening round of a golf tournament, I was able to transfer my frustrations to poor Charlie Brown. And when Charlie Brown has tried to analyze his own difficulties in life, he has always been able to express them best in sports terms.

During my senior year in high school, my mother showed me an ad that read: "Do you like to draw? Send in for our free talent test." This was my introduction to Art Instruction Schools, Inc., the correspondence school known at that time as Federal Schools. It was and still is located in Minneapolis, and even though, after signing up for the course, I could have taken my drawings there in person, I did all of the lessons by mail, as I would have had I lived several states away, for I was not that proud of my work.

I could have gone to one of several resident schools in the Twin Cities, but it was this correspondence course's emphasis upon cartooning that won me. The entire course came to approximately $170, and I remember my father having difficulty keeping up with the payments. I recall being quite worried when he received dunning letters, and when I expressed these worries to him he said not to become too concerned. I realized then that during those later Depression days he had become accustomed to owing people money. I eventually completed the course, and he eventually paid for it.

The two years following high school were extremely difficult, for this was the time that my mother was suffering so much with her illness. I was drafted during the month of February, in 1943, and spent several weeks at the induction center at Fort Snelling, Minnesota. We were allowed to go home on the weekends, and I recall how one Sunday evening, just before I had to return to Fort Snelling across the river from St. Paul, I went into the bedroom to say goodbye to my mother. She was lying in bed, very ill, and she said to me, "Yes, I suppose we should say good-bye because we probably never will see each other again." She died the next day and our tiny family was torn apart. I was shipped down to Camp Campbell, Kentucky, and my dad was left to try to put his life back together.

He continued to work daily in the barbershop and finally accumulated a total of forty-five years working in the same place.

All of the summer-camp ideas that I have drawn are a result of my having absolutely no desire as a child to be sent away to a summer camp. To me, that was equivalent to being drafted. When World War II came along, I met it with the same lack of enthusiasm. The three years I spent in the army taught me all I needed to know about loneliness, and my sympathy for the loneliness that all of us experience is dropped heavily upon poor Charlie Brown. I know what it is to have to spend days, evenings, and weekends by myself, and I also know how uncomfortable anxiety can be. I worry about almost all there is in life to worry about, and because I worry, Charlie Brown has to worry. I suppose our anxieties increase as we become responsible for more people. Perhaps some form of maturity should take care of this, but in my case it didn't. At any rate, I place the source of many of my problems on those three years in the army. The lack of any timetable or any idea as to when any of us would get out was almost unbearable. We used to sit around in the evenings and talk about things like this, and we were completely convinced that we were going to be in for the rest of our lives. The war seemed to have no end in sight. Yet, in spite of this, I recall a particular evening when I was on guard duty at the motor pool at the far end of the camp that is now called Fort Campbell, in the southern part of Kentucky; it was a beautiful summer evening, there was no one around in this area of the camp, and it was my job simply to see that no one interfered with any of the vehicles in that part of the motor pool, or tried to take any of them out of that particular gate. The only person in the world I had to worry about was my father, and I knew that he could take care of himself. As I sat there in the tiny guard shack, I seemed to be at complete peace with the world. Still, I knew for sure that I did not want to be where I was.

My mind has gone back to that hour many times, and I have tried to analyze why I should have been so at peace at that time. This is the kind of examination that produces some of the pages in Peanuts, but of course it is covered up by little cartoon characters, using dialogue that is at once condensed and exaggerated. Why does the cartoonist see something funny in all of these anxieties? Is it because the cartoonist is afraid of complete commitment? Perhaps this is why so many draw about political or social problems rather than try to run for political office or participate in social work. Perhaps it demonstrates a certain character trait, as with the person who makes what starts out to be a serious statement, but then, realizing what he has said, qualifies it or steps back slightly, adding a self-conscious chuckle.

When I was just out of high school, I started to submit cartoons to most of the major magazines, as all ambitious ama-

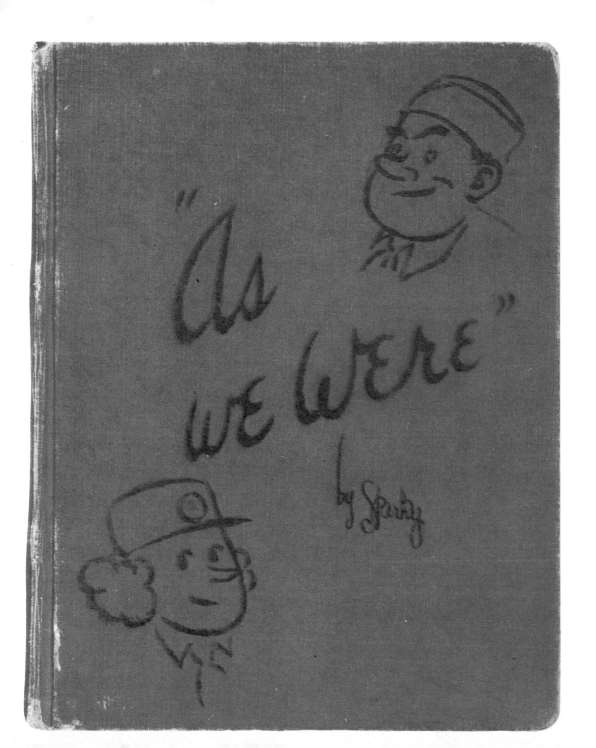

When I knew I was going into the army, I had a friend of mine who was a bookbinder make up a special sketchbook for me. I carried it with me for three years, although I didn't use it as much as I should have. The snapshot was taken during a six-week period when I was living in the corner of a stable near Rouen, France.

23

All but the last of these sketches were done at Camp Campbell and on maneuvers through northern Tennessee . . .

The other was made in the countryside of France. (Our division did not land in France until February, 1945.) I greatly admired the work being done by artists for Yank *magazine during these years, but realized that I had a long way to go before I would reach their standard.*

teurs do, but received only the ordinary rejection slips and no encouragement. After World War II, however, I set about in earnest to sell my work. I visited several places in the Twin Cities to try to get some job in whatever art department might be able to use my limited talents, but I was unsuccessful. I was almost hired one day to letter tombstones and was glad when the man did not call me back the next day, for I had already begun to worry what my friends might say when I told them about my new job. One day, however, with my collection of sample comic strips in hand, I visited the offices of Timeless Topix, the publishers of a series of Catholic comic magazines. The art director, Roman Baltes, seemed to like my lettering and said, "I think I may have something for you to do." He gave me several comic-book pages that had already been drawn by others but with the balloons left blank, and he told me that I should fill in the dialogue. This was my first job, but soon after I took it I was also hired by Art Instruction. For the next year, I lettered comic pages for Timeless Topix, working sometimes until past midnight, getting up early the next morning, taking a streetcar to downtown St. Paul, leaving the work outside the door of Mr. Baltes's office, and then going over to Minneapolis to work at the correspondence school.

My job there was to correct some of the basic lessons, and it introduced me to a roomful of people who did much to affect my later life. The instructors at this correspondence school were bright, and the atmosphere in the large room was invigorating. Each person there seemed to have a special interest in some phase of commercial art or cartooning, and some even in painting. The head of the department was Walter J. Wilwerding, a famous magazine illustrator of that period. Directly in front of me sat a man named Frank Wing who had drawn a special feature called "Yesterdays," which ran for a short time during the 1930s. He was a perfectionist at drawing things as they appeared, and I believe he did much to inspire me. He taught me the importance of drawing accurately, and even though I felt he was somewhat disappointed in me—and disapproved of my eventual drawing style—there is no doubt that I learned much from him. Almost nothing I draw now, in what is sometimes a quite extreme style, is not based on a real knowledge of how to draw that object, whether it be a shoe, a doghouse, or a child's hand. Cartooning, after all, is simply good design. In learning how to design a human hand after knowing how to draw it properly, one produces a good cartoon.

Some of the people who worked at Art Instruction Schools with me have remained friends all of these years, and I have used the names of several in the strip. Charlie Brown was named after my very good friend, Charlie Brown, whose desk was across the room. I recall perfectly the day he came over and first looked at the little cartoon face that had been named

26

Twenty-four years old and an instructor at Art Instruction Schools

after him. "Is that what he looks like?" he expressed with dismay. The characters of Linus and Frieda were also named after friends of mine who were instructors.

Those were days filled with hilarity, for there was always someone with a good joke, or laughter from some innocent mistake made by one of the students. It was not unusual for us to receive drawings of thumbs, and whenever we pulled such a drawing from its envelope we realized that once again a student had misunderstood the expression "making a thumbnail sketch." Another confusion came over the instruction to "experiment with matchstick figures"; students would actually send paper matchsticks glued to a sheet of paper.

There were many of us on the staff of Art Instruction who had ambitions to go on to other things, and I used my spare time, after completing the regular lesson criticisms, to work on my own cartoons. I tried never to let a week go by without having something in the mail working for me. During one period of time, from 1948 to 1950, I submitted cartoons regularly to the *Saturday Evening Post,* and sold fifteen of them. I was never able to break into any of the other magazines.

These were strongly formative years, and my ability to think of ideas and to present them properly was improving steadily. It seemed that it would be only a matter of time before I would be able to sell some type of marketable feature to a syndicate. I am still convinced that my eventual success was due largely to what I have called "the invigorating at-mosphere" in the department of instruction at the correspondence school. I suppose it would be similar to that of a newspaper office. I had always dreamed of someday having a desk in a newspaper office, but it never came about.

It was an exciting time for me because I was involved in the very sort of thing I wished to do. I not only lettered the complete Timeless Topix in English, but would do the French and Spanish translations without having any idea as to what the balloons were saying. One day Roman bought a page of little panel cartoons that I had drawn and titled "Just Keep Laughing." One of the cartoons showed a small boy who looked prophetically like Schroeder sitting on the curb with a baseball bat in his hands talking to a little girl who looked prophetically like Patty. He was saying, "I think I could learn to love you, Judy, if your batting average was a little higher." Frank Wing, my fellow instructor at Art Instruction, said, "Sparky, I think you should draw more of those little kids. They are pretty good." So I concentrated on creating a group of samples and eventually sold them as a weekly feature called "Li'l Folks" to the St. Paul *Pioneer Press.*

I was making regular trips to Chicago to try to sell a comic feature and was always gratified to talk with Mr. John Dille, Jr., at his National Newspaper Syndicate, for he was invariably kind and patient with me. This was not always true at some of the other syndicates. I dropped into the Chicago *Sun* one day and showed my work to Walt Ditzen, who was then

Timeless Topix, a Catholic comic magazine, bought two of my pages of gag cartoons with the promise of a monthly feature. After the second one, however, the priest in charge changed his mind. It was quite evident here that my style was beginning to develop, although these were done with a brush rather than a pen.

their comic editor, and he was very impressed with what he saw. I recall him exclaiming, ''I certainly cannot say no to this. We'll have to take it in to the president.'' We went into the man's office; he barely looked at the work and abruptly said ''No.''

At this time I was also becoming a little more gregarious and was learning how to talk with people. When I first used to board the morning Zephyr and ride it to Chicago, I would make the entire trip without talking to anyone. Little by little, however, I was getting rid of my shyness and feelings of in-

I drew this small cartoon in 1948. Although I realized it was against all the rules of professionalism, I sent the finished drawing to the Saturday Evening Post. *(Submissions to such magazines were usually done in rough form and were sent in batches of approximately ten to fifteen.) Several days later I received a note in the mail that said: ''Check Tuesday for spot drawing of boy on lounge.'' I was so used to having my work rejected that I thought the note meant that I should check my mailbox on Tuesday, that*

CHARLES SCHULZ

THE SATURDAY EVENING POST

they were going to send the drawing back. A couple of hours later I figured it out and, of course, was ecstatic. This was my first sale to a major market.

feriority, and learning how to strike up acquaintances on the train and talk to people. Two conversations in the dining car remain with me. I was seated across from a nicely, but conservatively, dressed gentleman one time on my way to Chicago; we introduced ourselves, and he asked me about the nature of my trip. After I had explained a little about myself, he told me that he was a Methodist minister, to which I replied, ''Yes, I sort of figured you were a minister.'' As I was saying this I knew, as we all too frequently do in such situations, that I was saying the wrong thing, but it came out before I could stop myself. Then, of course, I had to explain why I had deduced that he was a minister without offending him, even though the conclusion could be just as flattering as insulting. On my return trip to St. Paul, I struck up a conversation with another extremely interesting man who turned out to be the publisher of a small music magazine. Because I was just beginning to become acquainted with classical music, and because I was so interested in the entire subject, yet so clearly a layman, I had much to ask him. I had recently purchased Berlioz's *Harold in Italy,* and had fallen in love with its many melodic passages. I asked him what he thought of *Harold in Italy.* He considered this for several moments before looking at me and saying, ''Well, the human ear is a strange thing.'' I didn't dare ask him what he meant. I had the feeling it would be better not to know.

I continued to mail my work out to major syndicates. One

CHARLES M. SCHULZ
THE SATURDAY EVENING POST

"We're close enough. . . . Let's try for a field goal!"

I was encouraged by the Post's continuing acceptance of my work, and some of the cartoons the magazine bought over the two years before Peanuts got under way can be seen today in a somewhat prophetic light.

31

"Li'l Folks" was drawn for the Sunday St. Paul Pioneer Press, and starting in 1947 it ran for two years in the women's section. By then I had begun to sell my cartoons to the Post, and so I felt ready to ask the St. Paul editor for a better position in his paper

or for daily exposure. I even asked him if I could have more money. When he turned me down on all three counts, I suggested that perhaps I had better quit. He merely stated "All right." Thus endeth my career at the St. Paul Pioneer Press.

day I opened up a letter from one syndicate that turned me down, and then opened another letter from the director of NEA in Cleveland saying he liked my work very much. Arrangements were made during the next few months for me to start drawing a Sunday feature for NEA, but at the last minute their editors changed their minds and I had to start all over. In the spring of 1950 I accumulated a batch of some of the better cartoons I had been drawing for the St. Paul paper and mailed them off to United Feature Syndicate in New York. I don't know how much time went by without my hearing from them, but I'm sure it was at least six weeks. Convinced that my drawings had been lost in the mail, I finally wrote them a letter, describing the drawings I had sent and asking them if they could recall receiving anything similar. If not, I wanted to know so that I could put a tracer on the lost cartoons. Instead, I received a very nice letter from Jim Freeman, their editorial director, who said they were very interested in my work and would I care to come to New York and talk about it.

That was an exciting trip. When I arrived at the Syndicate offices early in the morning, no one other than the receptionist was there. I had brought along a new comic strip I had been working on, rather than the panel cartoons that United Feature had seen. I simply wanted to give them a better view of my work. I told the receptionist that I had not had breakfast yet, so I would go out and eat and then return. When I got back to the Syndicate offices they had already opened up the package I had left there and, in that short time, had decided they would rather publish the strip than the panel. This made me very happy, for I preferred the strip myself. I returned to Minneapolis filled with great hope for the future and asked a certain little girl to marry me. When she turned me down and married someone else, there was no doubt that Charlie Brown was on his way. Losers get started early.

October 2, 1950

When Peanuts began in
1950, there were only four
characters in the strip:
Patty, Charlie Brown,
Shermy, and Snoopy. I was
not sure which one would
eventually become the lead,
but the personalities soon
took care of that, although,
for several months, Charlie
Brown did not become the
put-upon character that he
is now. Patty and Shermy stayed with
the strip for a while, but Shermy fell
into the role of a straight man, and all
of the good lines eventually were given
to Charlie Brown or to one of the other
characters. Even Patty soon fell back
and became a straight character, along with
a new girl with a ponytail whose name was
Violet. I was never tempted to have Snoopy talk,
but gradually it became important that he do
some kind of thinking, and perhaps this was
where the strip turned its first important corner.
When Snoopy began to think, he took on a
personality that was very different from that of
any previous cartoon dog. He was slightly
superior to the kids in the strip, although he did
suffer a few defeats; you might say, at his own
paws. But most of the time he won out over

the kids. When Lucy was introduced into the strip she was a very tiny girl with circular eyes, which I abandoned at the suggestion of Jim Freeman. He said they gave her too much of a doll-like appearance, and he was right. So I cut the circles in half, and she and her brother, Linus, who came along later, now are the only characters to have tiny half-circles on each side of their eyes. These give them the appearance of being slightly out of focus, and if you have to say something about Lucy, this is as kind a way of putting it as possible.

When the early strips are seen now in reprinted collections, they are judged, unfortunately, by the strip as it is today. What has to be realized is that the characters I drew then came out of a style of gag cartooning that was prevalent at the time: tiny children looking up at huge adults and saying very sophisticated things. This was the professional school from which I graduated and which formed my style, and it took me several years to break away and develop a style of drawing that would allow the characters to do new and special things.

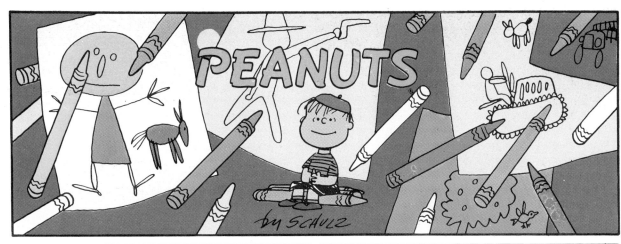

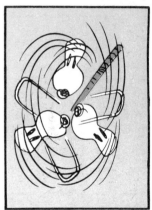

9-6

THUS ENDETH THE CROQUET GAME!

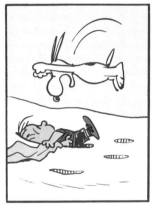

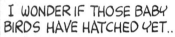

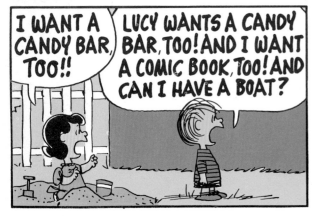

PEANUTS
featuring "Good ol' Charlie Brown"
by Schulz

HELLO, KITE-EATING TREE!

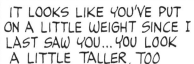

IT LOOKS LIKE YOU'VE PUT ON A LITTLE WEIGHT SINCE I LAST SAW YOU... YOU LOOK A LITTLE TALLER, TOO

BUT YOU HAVEN'T HAD ANY KITES LATELY, HAVE YOU?

WELL, YOU'RE NOT GOING TO GET **THIS** KITE, YOU DIRTY KITE-EATING TREE! I'LL FLY IT CLEAR OVER ON THE OTHER SIDE OF TOWN JUST TO SPITE YOU! YOU CAN STARVE, DO YOU HEAR?!

YOU'RE PRACTICALLY DROOLING, AREN'T YOU? YOU HAVEN'T EATEN A KITE FOR MONTHS, AND YOU'RE JUST DYING TO GET HOLD OF THIS ONE, AREN'T YOU? AREN'T YOU?

WELL, YOU'RE NOT, DO YOU HEAR ME? YOU'RE NOT!

HERE.. TAKE IT

IT'S BEEN A LONG WINTER, AND I'M VERY TENDER-HEARTED..

CHOMP! CHOMP! CHOMP!

12/24/67—Plate 21

PEANUTS
featuring
"Good ol' CharlieBrown"
by Schulz

I'M GOING TO TELL YOU SOMETHING I'VE NEVER TOLD ANYONE BEFORE...

DO YOU SEE THAT HILL OVER THERE?

SOMEDAY, I'M GOING TO GO OVER THAT HILL, AND FIND THE ANSWER TO MY DREAMS...

SOMEDAY I'M GOING TO GO OVER THAT HILL, AND FIND HAPPINESS AND FULFILLMENT...

I THINK THAT, FOR ME, ALL THE ANSWERS TO LIFE LIE BEYOND THOSE CLOUDS AND OVER THE GRASSY SLOPES OF THAT HILL!

5-26

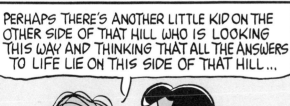

PERHAPS THERE'S ANOTHER LITTLE KID ON THE OTHER SIDE OF THAT HILL WHO IS LOOKING THIS WAY AND THINKING THAT ALL THE ANSWERS TO LIFE LIE ON THIS SIDE OF THAT HILL...

FORGET IT, KID!

Schulz

10/13/68—Plate 30

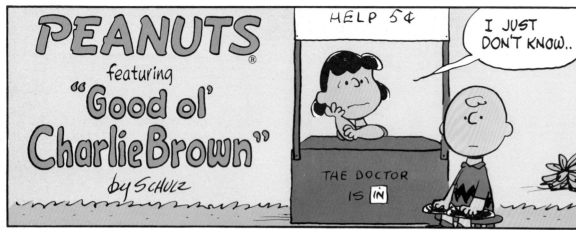

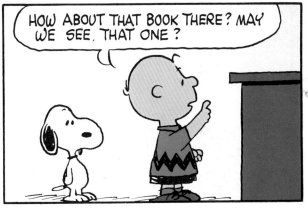

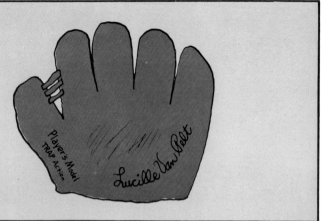

PEANUTS
featuring "Good ol' Charlie Brown"
by Schulz

THREE MINUTES TO PLAY...

HERE'S THE WORLD-FAMOUS QUARTERBACK COMING OFF THE BENCH TO WIN THE BIG GAME...

11-23

SIXTEEN! FORTY-TWO! SEVEN! HUT!!

HE FADES BACK, AND SPOTS AN OPEN RECEIVER...

HE HURLS THE BOMB!

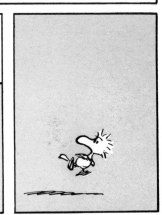

BONK!

BAD HANDS!

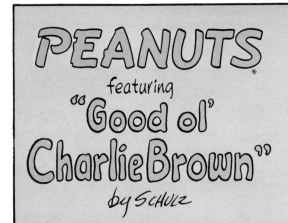

2 The initial theme of Peanuts was based on the cruelty that exists among children. I recall all too vividly the struggle that takes place out on the playground. This is the struggle that adults grow away from and seem to forget about. Adults learn to protect themselves. In this day of organized sports for children, we forget how difficult it once was for smaller children to set up any kind of ball game at a playground because so often there were older and bigger kids to interrupt the fun. I have always despised bullies, and even though someone once suggested that I have much psychological bullying going on in Peanuts, I do consciously try to stay away from that sort of thing.

As the strip progressed from the fall of the year 1950, the characters began to change. Charlie Brown was a flippant little guy, who soon turned into the loser he is known as today. This was the first of the formulas to develop. Formulas are truly the backbone of the comic strip. In fact, they are probably the backbone of any continuing entertainment. As Charlie Brown developed, so did characters such as Lucy, Schroeder, and Linus. Snoopy was the slowest to develop, and it was his eventually walking around on two feet that turned him into a lead character. It has certainly been difficult to keep him from taking over the feature.

There are various origins for the characters. Charlie Brown is supposed to represent what is sometimes called ''everyman.'' When I was small, I believed that my face was so bland

that people would not recognize me if they saw me some place other than where they normally would. I was sincerely surprised if I happened to be in the downtown area of St. Paul, shopping with my mother, and we would bump into a fellow student at school, or a teacher, and they recognized me. I thought that my ordinary appearance was a perfect disguise. It was this weird kind of thinking that prompted Charlie Brown's round, ordinary face. Linus came from a drawing that I made one day of a face almost like the one he now has. I experimented with some wild hair, and I showed the sketch to a friend of mine who sat near me at Art Instruction whose name was Linus Maurer. He thought it was kind of funny, and we both agreed it might make a good new character for the strip. It seemed appropriate that I should name the character Linus. It also seemed that Linus would fit very well as Lucy's younger brother. Lucy had already been in the strip for about a year, and had immediately developed her fussbudget personality. We called our oldest daughter, Meredith, a fussbudget when she was very small, and from this I applied the term to Lucy. Schroeder was named after a young boy with whom I used to caddy at Highland Park golf course in St. Paul. I don't recall ever knowing his first name, but just Schroeder seemed right for the character in the strip, even before he became the great musician he now is.

One night, over ten years after I began drawing Peanuts, I had a dream in which I created a new character whose name was a combination of Mexican and Swedish. Why in the world I had such a dream and would think of such a name as Jose Peterson is a mystery to me. Most of the time, things that are a complete riot when you are dreaming are not the least bit funny when you wake up. In this case, however, it seemed like a good idea, so I developed a story about the arrival of Jose Peterson in the neighborhood, and he has remained ever since, usually playing on Peppermint Patty's baseball team.

Patty has been a good addition for me, and I think she could almost carry another strip by herself. A dish of candy sitting in our living room inspired her name. At the time I was thinking of writing a series of children's books completely separate from the Peanuts strip, but my schedule kept me too busy to ever get started and almost a year went by before I decided that I had better use this name, lest someone else think of it and beat me to it. So in this case I created the character to fit the name, and Peppermint Patty came into being. Her little friend, Marcie, who is always addressing her as "Sir," has also been a good addition to the strip.

I have always believed that you not only cast a strip to enable the characters to do things you want them to, but that the characters themselves, by their very nature and personality, should provide you with ideas. These are the characters who remain in the feature and are seen most often. The more distinct the personalities are, the better the feature will be. Readers can then respond to the characters as though they were real.

It is interesting to observe that many of the lead characters in our most successful comic strips have had similar personalities. Readers are generally sympathetic toward a lead character who is rather gentle, sometimes put upon, and not always the brightest person. Perhaps this is the kind of person who is easiest to love. I really don't know. It may also be that giving the supporting characters the most distinct personalities makes for a more controllable story. A character with more of a "middle ground" personality can hold the rest of the group together. In the case of Peanuts, I like to have Charlie Brown eventually be the focal point of almost every story. No matter what happens to any of the other characters, somehow Charlie Brown is involved at the end and usually is the one who brings disaster upon one of his friends or receives the brunt of the blow. Chralie Brown has to be the one who suffers, because he is a caricature of the average person. Most of us are much more acquainted with losing than we are with winning. Winning is great, but it isn't funny. While one person is a happy winner, there may be a hundred losers using funny stories to console themselves.

Snoopy's appearance and personality have changed probably more than those of any of the other characters. As my drawing style loosened, Snoopy was able to do more things,

and when I finally developed the formula of using his imagination to dream of being many heroic figures, the strip took on a completely new dimension. I had observed that there were many neighborhood dogs that seemed almost smarter than the children who were their masters. The dogs seemed to tolerate the silly things the kids did; they seemed to be very wise. This was one of the initial themes of Snoopy that I have built upon in many ways. Snoopy refuses to be caught in the trap of doing ordinary things like chasing and retrieving sticks, and he refuses to take seriously his role as the devoted dog who greets his master when he returns home from school. In recent years, I have played up the gag that he doesn't even remember his master's name, but simply thinks of him as "that round-headed kid."

One of the questions most frequently asked of a cartoonist seems to be: "Where do you get your ideas?" After twenty-five years of drawing the Peanuts comic strip, I feel that I have learned a good deal about creativity and how one prepares an idea. Still rather a mystery to me is where some of the little phrases come from, and why it is possible to think of ten ideas in one day, and not be able to think of a single one the next. Perhaps I would be better off simply saying that I don't know how I think of all these ideas, which would be the same kind of answer I frequently give people who say, "I just want to let you know how much I admire your philosophy." This is a statement that continually baffles me, for I sincerely do not know what they mean. Therefore, all I can do is say "Thank you." I am always tempted, however, to start some kind of discussion to find out just what it is they really admire.

Some of my ideas can be traced back. I have drawn many cartoons showing the children standing in line to buy tickets to a movie, because my memories of Saturday afternoons at the Park Theater in St. Paul are so vivid. Almost nothing could prevent us from seeing the latest episode of the Saturday afternoon serial and the movie that followed. One day, the theater advertised that the first 500 customers would receive a free Butterfinger candy bar. I must have been the 501st child in line, because when I got up to the window, the man said, "Sorry, that's all there is." Forty years later, I had the same thing happen to Charlie Brown. The shape of the theater itself inspired another Sunday page (plate 45). Charlie Brown is talking about how things change as we grow older. Of course I used his father as the instrument for my own recollections, and his father has apparently told him how the theater that he attended when he was a small boy seemed to get narrower and narrower as the years went by. This is similar to going back to a house where you once lived when you were young, and discovering that the backyard you remember as being so large is really absurdly small. Another time, Charlie Brown's father, also using my memory, recalls a cute little girl he used to know (plate 46). When he picked her up in his 1934 black two-door sedan, she reached over and

locked the driver's side of the car before he could get back around to his side of the car. She then sat there and grinned at him. These are the little jokes that make new love such a joy, and even though Peppermint Patty is not able to understand it, Charlie Brown instinctively knows that those moments should be cherished. Charlie Brown has also defined security as being able to sleep in the back seat of your parents' car (plate 47). This, again, is a childhood memory, one supported by many readers who have told me that they also recall the wonderful joy of doing this with a feeling of complete security when returning home late at night. The shattering blow comes in later years when one realizes that this can never happen again. Adults are doomed to ride in the front seat forever.

Probably one of the biggest defeats any of us can experience in this life is being turned down by the girl we love, and then seeing her turn around and almost immediately marry someone else. This is a defeat from which it is almost impossible to recover. Charlie Brown's defeats, of course, are a caricature. None of us suffers the continual agony he does because his life is caricatured to the same degree that he is drawn. I have memories of a little girl, which have been translated into many defeats for Charlie Brown. He is talking in one particular page about an episode related to him and his family (plate 48). It seems that his father and the girl had spent a wonderful day together having a picnic, and then going to a movie. The father tells how this movie had impressed him very much, and how afterward whenever he saw Anne Baxter in other films it would always take him back to that wonderful day he spent with the girl he loved. When telling a friend about it, however, the friend says, "Why, that was not Anne Baxter in the movie, it was Susan Hayward." This is how my own memories become mixed up with the memories of Charlie Brown's fictional father. For years, the sight of Anne Baxter on a late-late show or in a movie depressed me, for it brought back memories of that day, and that evening, and my defeat. And when someone told me that I had been depressed by the wrong fact all those years, it came as quite a shock.

Life has many finalities, and readers being able to make their own interpretations is, I suppose, what makes a cartoon idea successful. I frequently keep little scraps of paper in one of my desk drawers with slight notations for ideas that I hope someday to put together into a workable strip. One that I thought about for over a year eventually became one of the most sought-after pages I have ever done. We have received countless requests for the original and for reprints. It all started when my oldest son, Monte, was in high school and was involved with an art class where the project was a coathanger sculpture. He was telling me about it one day while we were riding home in the car from school, and he said that he was going to transform a coat hanger into the figure of a baseball pitcher. It sounded like a good idea to me, and I was

anxious to hear about the final results. Several weeks went by before he mentioned it again, and this time he told me that the teacher had handed back the projects and he had received a *C* on his coat-hanger sculpture. I remember being quite disturbed by this, because I could not understand how a teacher was able to grade this kind of project. I thought about it as the months went by, and finally translated it into the Sunday page where Sally expresses her indignation over receiving the same grade for her piece of coat-hanger sculpture (plate 49). Her questions were the same ones that I had wanted to ask Monte's teacher. Had he judged the sculpture as a piece of art? If so, what criteria did he use to judge it? Was he grading the person on his ability to create this work of art? If so, what control did the person have over the talent that was given him at birth? Was the person being graded upon what he had learned in the project? If so, should the teacher not be willing to share in the grade? Sally made a good instrument for this kind of idea, for she is a character who expresses indignation well, and who is completely puzzled by all of the things she has to go through in school.

This, of course, is one of the secrets to casting a comic strip. It is much like casting a drama company, where you must have actors who can play whatever roles are called for. The comic strip itself should have a variety of personalities so that you are not always striking the same note. You must have a full keyboard on which to play out the themes and variations demanded each day. Lucy has been inviting Charlie Brown to come running up to kick the football and then pulling it away each year for eighteen years. Every time I complete this annual page, I am sure I will never be able to think of another one, but so far I have always managed to come up with a new twist for the finish. (I suppose I have been encouraged to keep it up during the last three or four years because California's ex-governor, Ronald Reagan, once told me that this was one of his favorite episodes, and I am easily flattered into continuing something if I have been told that it has been a favorite.) It all started, of course, with a childhood memory of being unable to resist the temptation to pull away the football at the kickoff. We all did it, we all fell for it. In fact, I was told by a professional football player that he actually saw it happen in a college game at the University of Minnesota. The Gophers were apparently leading by a good margin, everyone was enjoying himself, and the man holding the football, like the kids in the neighborhood, could not resist the temptation to pull it away. I wish I had been there to see it.

I have never been a very successful kite flyer and have used the excuse that I never lived where there were good areas to fly them. When I was growing up, we always lived in residential areas that had too many trees and too many telephone wires. Recollections of those handicaps inspired Charlie Brown's troubles with kite flying. As I grew older and tried to fly kites for my own children, I discovered that I still had the same problems. I observed that when a kite becomes caught in a tall tree, it is irretrievable and gradually disappears over a period of several weeks. Now obviously the kite had to go someplace, so it seemed to me that the tree must be eating it. This is how the series developed about Charlie Brown's violent battles with his local "kite-eating tree."

When my daughter Amy had her fifteenth birthday, I gave her a dozen roses and told her that she would soon be a beautiful young lady and that the boys would be calling on her and probably would be bringing her presents. I told her that I wanted to be the first one in her life to give her a dozen roses. This was the inspiration for the Sunday page that showed Peppermint Patty receiving roses from her father on her birthday. For several years, I have referred to our youngest daughter, Jill, as a "rare gem," so I simply combined our two daughters into one and created the very sentimental page that concludes with Peppermint Patty saying, "Suddenly, I feel very feminine" (plate 50).

I suppose my long-time interest in music enabled me to carry out the ideas involving Schroeder playing his toy piano. This interest was kept alive by several of my friends at Art Instruction. We all collected classical albums, which we frequently shared on evenings when we got together to listen to music and challenge each other in wild games of hearts. Having been fascinated for several months by Strauss waltzes, I graduated one day to the purchase of Beethoven's Second

Symphony, and I remember that this record opened up a whole new world for me.

A toy piano that we had bought for our oldest daughter, Meredith, eventually became the piano that Schroeder uses for his daily practicing. Seeing a portion of Beethoven's Ninth Symphony in print gave me the idea for the many episodes involving Schroeder's admiration for that great composer. I have been asked many times: "Why Beethoven?" The answer is simply that it is funnier that way. There are certain words and certain names that work better than others. I don't believe it would be half as funny if Schroeder admired Brahms. There is also the very practical fact that to most of us laymen, Beethoven, Rembrandt, and Shakespeare are the three mountain peaks in music, art, and literature. I have read several biographies of Beethoven—being strangely fascinated by the lives of composers, much more so than by the lives of painters—and from these biographies have managed to come up with different things that have concerned Schroeder. For a long time I had thought that the sentence "Lobkowitz stopped his annunity" was an extremely funny sentence, and I was happy to find a way to use it (plate 51). Sometimes, drawing the musical scores that Schroeder plays can be very tedious, but I love the pattern that the notes make on the page. I have always tried to be authentic in this matter. I believe that some readers enjoy trying to determine what it is that Schroeder is playing.

Linus's blanket was inspired by the blankets that our first

PEANUTS
featuring
"Good ol' Charlie Brown"
by Schulz

HEY, CHUCK, COME ON OVER, AND SEE WHAT MY DAD GAVE ME FOR MY BIRTHDAY..

ROSES!

WOW!

AND YOU KNOW WHAT HE SAID?

10-4

HE SAID THAT I'M GROWING UP FAST, AND SOON I'LL BE A BEAUTIFUL YOUNG LADY, AND ALL THE BOYS WILL BE CALLING ME UP SO HE JUST WANTED TO BE THE FIRST ONE IN MY LIFE TO GIVE ME A DOZEN ROSES!

HE CALLS ME "A RARE GEM"

YOUR DAD LIKES YOU... HAPPY BIRTHDAY..

SUDDENLY, I FEEL VERY FEMININE!

three children dragged around the house, and the character of "Joe Cool," as expressed through Snoopy, evolved out of something that my second son, Craig, mentioned when I overheard a conversation between him and some other teenagers at our ice arena. Craig is also the inspiration for one of the more recent series involving "Joe Motocross."

My son Monte claims to have been the one who gave me the idea for Snoopy chasing the Red Baron in his World War I flying gear while atop his "Sopwith Camel" doghouse. I, of course, deny that he actually gave me the idea, but I will admit that he inspired it, for at the time he was very much involved with building plastic models of World War I airplanes. It was on an afternoon when he was showing me one of his models that I drew a helmet on Snoopy and placed him in a pilot's pose on top of his doghouse. The whole thing kind of fit together. You might say it simply took off, and I knew I had one of the best things I had thought of in a long time. In fact, this theme went on for several years and even produced two separate books.

Direct ideas have been much more rare. Our youngest daughter, Jill, came up to me one day and said, "I just discovered something. If you hold your hands upside down, you get the opposite of what you pray for." I used this as an idea exactly as she said it. Craig also told me one day that a good way to clean one's fingernails was to use toothpaste. Again, I used the idea almost the way he said it. Another

time our second daughter, Amy, provided me with an idea that I think came out as well as any I have ever drawn. The entire family was around the dinner table and, for some reason, Amy seemed particularly noisy that evening. After putting up with this for about ten minutes, I turned to her and said, "Amy, couldn't you be quiet for just a little while?" She said nothing, but picked up a piece of bread and began to butter it with a knife and asked, "Am I buttering too loud for you?" This was very easily translated into a Linus and Lucy Sunday page.

In going through hundreds of Sunday pages that I have drawn over the years, I was startled to discover that the year 1968 produced a sudden turn in new ideas. For some reason, I was able to come up with a whole flock of new themes that I had never worked on before. I have looked back to that year, but have been unable to discover what it might have been that caused me to be able to think of so many new ideas at that time. Generally speaking, it seems that more good cartoon ideas have come out of a mood of sadness than a feeling of well-being. A couple of years ago, some events in my life saddened me to such a degree that I could no longer listen to the car radio. I did not want to risk becoming depressed while riding alone in the car, and I found that almost everything I listened to on the car radio would send me into a deep depression. In spite of this, I was still able to come up with cartoon ideas that were not only as

good as anything I had ever done, but carried the strip forward into new areas.

At another earlier time, I had an album of Hank Williams songs to which I used to listen over and over. One night, saddened by the plaintive lyrics of a lost love, I created the first of a long series where Charlie Brown tried so desperately to get up the courage to speak to the little red-haired girl. It would be difficult to explain to someone how a Hank Williams song had prompted such thoughts, but this is the way it happened.

Not all of my ideas have worked out successfully. One day, while searching for some kind of new story to work on, I decided to have the character named Frieda, the little girl who is so proud of her naturally curly hair, threaten Snoopy with bringing a cat into the neighborhood. Snoopy was horrified and, when the cat arrived, did not like it at all. Fortunately for him, I also discovered that *I* didn't care much for the cat. For one thing, I realized that I don't draw a cat very well, and secondly, if I were to keep up the relationship, I would have a traditionally cat-and-dog strip, which was something I certainly wanted to avoid. The cat and the dog could not talk to each other because Snoopy never talks, he only thinks. So I would have had to show the cat and dog thinking to each other, which was totally unreasonable. More important, the cat brought Snoopy back to being too much of a real dog. By the time the cat had come into the strip, Snoopy was drifting further and further into his fantasy life, and it was important that he continue in that direction. To take him back to his earlier days would not work, so I did the obvious and removed the cat. (My only regret was that I had named the cat after Faron Young, a country-and-western singer whom I admired very much. This was the second time that a country-and-western singer had contributed something to the strip.) An offstage cat now works better than a real one in the same way that the little red-haired girl, Linus's blanket-hating grandmother, Charlie Brown's father, the barber, and the kids' teachers all work better in the reader's imagination. There comes a time when it is actually too late to draw these offstage characters. I would never be able to draw the little red-haired girl, for example, as well as the reader draws her in his imagination.

The early years of Peanuts contain many ideas that revolved around very tiny children, because my own children were still young at the time. As the strip grew, it took on a slight degree of sophistication, although I have never claimed to be the least sophisticated myself. But it also took on a quality that I think is even more important, and that is one which I can describe only as abstraction. The neighborhood in which the characters lived ceased gradually to be real. Snoopy's doghouse could function only if it were drawn from a direct side view. Snoopy himself had become a character so unlike a dog that he could no longer inhabit a real dog-house. And the cartooning of the other characters, with their large, round heads and tiny arms, came frequently to pro-hibit them from doing some of the more realistic things that a more normal style of cartooning would allow. Neverthe-less, this was the direction I wanted to take, and I believe it has led me to do some things that no one ever before attempted in a comic strip.

There are many standard poses that I use in the Peanuts drawings, and they are all used for definite reasons, some more important than others. I was always overly cautious with my own children, worrying constantly of their becoming injured, or worse, in some mishap. When I began to draw the kids in the strip talking to each other, the obvious pose was to show them sitting on the curb, reminiscent of the early "Skippy" strips, drawn by Percy Crosby. The characters in Peanuts, however, were much younger than Skippy and his friends, and I was always sensitive about showing them sitting on a street curb, where they could very easily get run over. Therefore, I always drew them sitting at the end of the front walk that ran down from the steps, out to the main sidewalk. This was not always a suitable pose for some of the later strips, so I eventually changed it to show them standing by a stone wall. This gave the reader a chance to speculate as to what the characters might be looking at while talking about life's problems and leaning in various posi-tions. I also gradually became aware that it was important for readers instantly to identify the characters and what they were doing. This is the main reason I have never gone in for using tricky camera angles and a variety of poses from panel to panel. For example, there would be no advantage to show Schroeder from a variety of views. It is much more important that the reader identify him immediately and have the feeling of familiarity as he sees him seated at his tiny toy piano. Admittedly, it would be difficult to draw some of these characters from different angles. In certain cases, they simply do not fit, and other poses are easier to fake from certain angles. When it comes right down to it, we have to get back to what looks best, and Schroeder looks best when drawn from side view, playing his piano. Also, I have always drawn the characters viewed from their own level, which gets the reader right down into the picture without any superior, adult view. I am probably the only cartoonist who always draws grass from side view.

The more Snoopy moved into his life of fantasy, the more important it became for his doghouse to remain in side view. You simply cannot have a dog doing and thinking the things that Snoopy does on a realistic doghouse. The image is much more acceptable when the doghouse is drawn only from the side. When necessary, it almost loses its identity completely. Snoopy's typewriter could never balance on the peak the way it does and, of course, Snoopy himself is somewhat of a mystery when one examines his sleeping pose closely. I once inquired of a veterinarian how birds stay on tree limbs when they fall asleep. He told me that their claws receive a message from their brain after they have fallen asleep, which tightens a certain muscle, keeping them from tumbling off the branch. He said a similar thing occurs to horses, allowing them to sleep while standing. Humans do not have this ability. When I am asked how Snoopy remains on top of his doghouse after falling asleep, I am now able to say that his brain sends a message to his ears, which lock him to the top of his doghouse.

The baseball scenes work wonderfully well even though we never see the other team. Most of the time we are focused on Charlie Brown, standing on top of the pitcher's mound. It was Robert Short, author of *The Gospel According to Peanuts,* who once reminded me that Charlie Brown's pose on the pitcher's mound was not unlike that of Job on his ash heap. He was quite surprised when I told him that this had never occurred to me.

Baseball has played a prominent role in the strip because it is effective when dealing with static situations. A violent sport, or one that contains a lot of action, does not lend itself to having characters standing around spouting philosophical opinions. There is also the element of tension, as in the sport of baseball itself. I can show Charlie Brown standing on the mound, and build up the tension of what is going to happen before the game begins or before he throws the next pitch. This would be difficult with almost any other sport.

The front-view pose of Linus holding his blanket is used for two reasons: again, for familiarity, and secondly, for practical reasons. With his large head and short arms, it would be very difficult to draw Linus sucking his thumb from side view, for he would have a hard time stretching his arm out that far. The animators in Hollywood, who have worked on our many television shows and movies, have discovered this much to their chagrin. There are some poses that simply have to be avoided.

The introduction of Woodstock into the strip is a good demonstration of how some things cannot work until they have been drawn properly. The little birds that had appeared earlier were drawn much too realistically to be able to fill humorous roles, but as I loosened up the drawing style, Woodstock gradually developed. A problem similar to that of the cat has now come about, and I have had to back off slightly. I would much prefer that Snoopy not communicate with Woodstock, but there are some ideas that are too important to abandon, so I have him speaking to Woodstock through "thought" balloons. I've held fast with Woodstock's means of communication, though it has been tempting at times to have him talk. I feel it would be a mistake to give in on this point, however, for I think it is more important that all of Woodstock's talking remain depicted simply in the little scratch marks that appear above his head.

If Peanuts has been unique in any way, it has been because of the absence of adults. I usually say that they do not appear because the daily strip is only an inch and a half high, and they wouldn't have room to stand up. Actually, they have been left out because they would intrude in a world where they could only be uncomfortable. Adults are not needed in the Peanuts strip. In earlier days I experimented with offstage voices, but soon abandoned this, as it was not only impractical but actually clumsy. Instead, I have developed a cast of offstage adults who are talked about, but never seen or heard. Charlie Brown's father seems to be a gentle soul who is developing a few problems. Charlie Brown once said that he saw him in the kitchen late one night looking at his high school annual, eating cold cereal, and looking very sad. This would say something about almost every one of us. Linus's blanket-hating grandmother has caused a good deal of trouble for poor Linus because she seems to be convinced that she can cure him of his terrible habit of having to drag around this spiritual blotter. When he knows that she is coming over to their house to visit, and realizing it is impossible to hide his blanket from her, he tucks it into a self-addressed envelope and drops it into the mail, knowing it will not come back for at least four or five days. Another strong character who never appears is Linus's teacher, Miss Othmar. Linus denies that he loves her, insisting he is simply "very fond of the ground on which she walks." I have often heard it said that children know a lot more about what is going on around them than adults are willing to admit. But I have also observed that children sometimes understand much less of what is going on around them than we think they do. For one thing, children seem to live more for themselves than do adults, and I see no reason why they should not. They frequently get a distorted view of what is actually happening. I pointed this out once in a little story about Linus and his teacher where he had been assigned to bring some eggshells to school for a project in which they were studying igloos. The eggshells were evidently to be placed in a setting where they would appear to be an Eskimo village. For some reason, Linus could not remember to bring the eggshells to school, and he noticed that Miss Othmar was very upset. Being very self-conscious, as most children are, he thought for sure that Miss Othmar was upset because of his inability to remember the eggshells. It turned out, however, that Miss Othmar merely was involved in an after-hours romance. Eventually she ran off to get married.

I am not sure, but I believe that in addition to being the first cartoonist to use authentic musical scores in his comic strip, I am also the first to use extensive theological references. I have done this in spite of severe criticism from people who have written to me saying that it is a desecration of the scriptures to quote them in "such a lowly thing as a newspaper comic strip." My mind reels with countless things I would like to write back to these people, but I always decide it is better not to say anything. These scriptural references have always been done with dignity and, of course, with much love, for I am extremely fond of studying both the Old and the New Testaments.

I received a letter one day from a young seminary student named Robert Short, who had been using some of the Peanuts material as part of his thesis. He asked permission to have this material published in book form. I appreciated many of the things he said in his thesis, though I realized that when dealing with religious opinions, you are leaving yourself open for all kinds of criticism and trouble. I told him that I would certainly be pleased if his book were published, but I wanted no one to think that we had collaborated on his work. This is my philosophy: Always accept the compliments and praise, but avoid the blame. As it turned out, *The Gospel According to Peanuts* was a tremendous best-seller and did much good. It opened the way for Bob to tour the country and speak to thousands of college students, as it opened the way in a similar manner for other religious workers to lead discussion groups.

While I have introduced many theological themes into Peanuts, I have also been aware that it is unfair to subscribing newspaper editors to promote views that can become too personal. I do believe, however, that it is quite possible to use the scriptures in a gentle manner in a comic strip. My own theological views have changed considerably over the past twenty-five years, and I now shy away from anyone who claims to possess all of the truth. I do not find it easy to discuss with an interviewer things of a spiritual nature, for they do not always come out on the printed page in a manner that can be easily understood. I find it much safer, as well as more gratifying, to reserve theological discussions for a time when you can look the other person directly in the eye. There are too many "howevers" that need to be spoken when discussing subjects this sensitive, and they simply do not come out well in the average magazine or newspaper interview.

Every profession and every type of work has its difficulties, and one of the most difficult aspects of creating a comic strip is attempting to sustain a certain quality on a day-to-day schedule that never ends. Trying not only to maintain that level, but to improve the feature as the months go by, in spite of the problems one may be having in one's life, makes cartooning a very demanding profession. I believe the ability to sustain a certain quality, in spite of everything, is one of the elements that separates the good features from the weaker ones. I went through one strange phase in my life when I became quite disturbed by dreams, which occurred to me irregularly over a period of several weeks. I would find in my dreams that I was crying uncontrollably, and when I awakened, I was extremely depressed. Naturally, it is not easy to disregard something like this, to forget it all and start thinking of funny cartoons, for the daily pressures of life affect us all. I have talked to many people who have agreed that they find themselves feeling angry throughout much of the day. The mere routine of having to deal with customers or company people in superior positions is enough to make the working day difficult. Sometimes, simply reading the morning paper, or watching the television news, is enough to discourage anyone. We become angry with ourselves, with our family, our fellow workers, with people we meet in stores, and, of course, with the government. It takes a good deal of maturity to be able to set all this anger aside and carry on with your daily work.

PEANUTS
featuring
"Good ol' Charlie Brown"
by Schulz

I APPRECIATE YOUR TAKING ME ALONG TO PLAY TENNIS, LINUS...

THAT'S THE ONLY TROUBLE WITH TENNIS.. YOU CAN'T PLAY IT ALONE

MAYBE WE WON'T GET TO PLAY AT ALL... THE COURTS ARE ALL FULL..

THE COURTS ARE ALWAYS FULL WITH BIG KIDS, AND THEY NEVER LET YOU PLAY... I HATE BIG KIDS! THEY NEVER GIVE YOU A CHANCE!

THEY'LL PLAY ALL DAY...JUST YOU WATCH! THEY'LL HOG THE COURTS ALL DAY! THEY'LL NEVER QUIT...THEY'LL JUST KEEP ON PLAYING AND PLAYING, AND THEY'LL NEVER...

YOU BIG KIDS GET OFF THAT COURT RIGHT NOW, OR MY BOY-FRIEND WILL CLOBBER YOU!!

7-18

THAT'S THE ONLY TROUBLE WITH TENNIS... YOU CAN'T PLAY IT ALONE

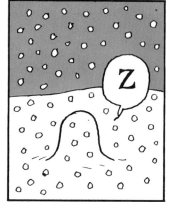

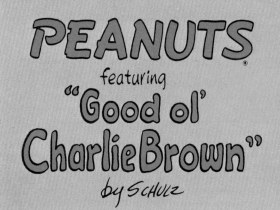
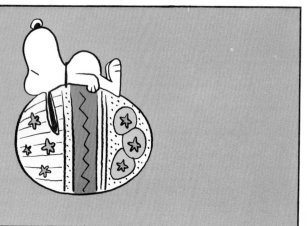

PEANUTS
featuring
"Good ol' CharlieBrown"
by Schulz

I HAVE A QUESTION..

WHAT DO YOU THINK THE SECRET OF LIVING IS, CHUCK?

THE SECRET OF LIVING IS TO OWN A CONVERTIBLE AND A LAKE..

A CONVERTIBLE AND A LAKE?

4-16

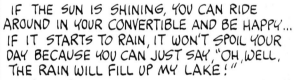

IF THE SUN IS SHINING, YOU CAN RIDE AROUND IN YOUR CONVERTIBLE AND BE HAPPY... IF IT STARTS TO RAIN, IT WON'T SPOIL YOUR DAY BECAUSE YOU CAN JUST SAY, "OH, WELL, THE RAIN WILL FILL UP MY LAKE!"

WHAT DO YOU THINK THE SECRET OF LIVING IS, SNOOPY?

SMAK!

A CONVERTIBLE AND A LAKE.. I DON'T KNOW ABOUT YOU, CHUCK...

IF YOUR LAKE IS DRYING UP, YOU CAN SAY, "OH, WELL, THIS IS NICE WEATHER FOR RIDING IN A CONVERTIBLE.."

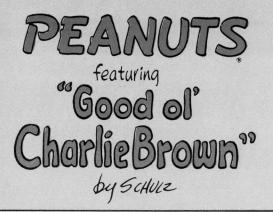

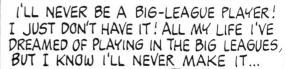

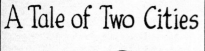

PEANUTS
featuring
"Good ol' CharlieBrown"
by SCHULZ

THAT WAS A GOOD DIVE..

HAD IT BEEN INTO MY WATER DISH, I WOULD EVEN CALL IT A BEAUTIFUL DIVE...HOWEVER, IT WAS NOT INTO MY WATER DISH... IT WAS INTO MY SUPPER DISH!

8-13

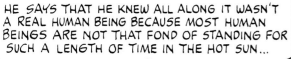

PEANUTS
featuring
"Good ol' Charlie Brown"
by Schulz

COLUMNIST

HERE'S ONE FROM IOWA...AND HERE'S ONE FROM PENNSYLVANIA..

Advice For Dog Owners

type type type

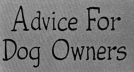

"DEAR SIR, I HAVE A DOG WHO CONTINUALLY SCRATCHES HIS EARS...WHAT SHOULD I DO? SIGNED, 'WONDERING'"

Dear Wondering, What I'm wondering is how you can be so dumb! Take your dog to the vet right away, stupid.

type type type type

"DEAR SIR, WE HAVE THREE PUPPIES WHO HAVE ENLARGED JOINTS AND ARE LAME... WHAT DO YOU THINK CAUSED THIS, AND WHAT SHOULD WE DO? SIGNED, 'DOG OWNER'"

9-24

Dear Dog Owner, Why don't you take up rock collecting? You're too stupid to be a dog owner. In the meantime, call your vet immediately.

type type type type

"DEAR SIR, MY DOG HAS BEEN COUGHING LATELY... WHAT SHOULD I DO? SIGNED, 'CONFUSED'"

Dear Confused, You're not confused, you're just not very smart. Now, you get that dog to the vet right away before I come over and punch you in the nose!

type type type

I WRITE A VERY FIRM COLUMN!

PEANUTS

featuring "Good ol' Charlie Brown"

by Schulz

WHAT A GREAT TITLE!

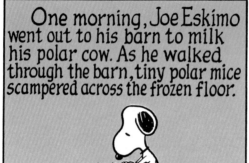

Toodle-oo, Caribou! A Tale of the Frozen North

One morning, Joe Eskimo went out to his barn to milk his polar cow. As he walked through the barn, tiny polar mice scampered across the frozen floor.

HMM..

I HATE TO TELL YOU THIS, BUT THERE ISN'T SUCH A THING AS A POLAR COW..

THERE ISN'T?

10-1

OKAY, SCRATCH THE POLAR COW..

THERE AREN'T SUCH THINGS AS POLAR MICE, EITHER...

THERE AREN'T?

OKAY, SCRATCH THE POLAR MICE... SIGH..

SOME OF MY BEST NOVELS NEVER GET OFF THE GROUND..

10/1/72—Plate 75

PEANUTS
featuring
"Good ol' Charlie Brown"
by SCHULZ

PEPPERMINT PATTY LOVES

LIFE IS LIKE A BRACELET, CHUCK

LIKE A WHAT?

LIFE IS LIKE A BRACELET... IT HAS LITTLE JEWELS AROUND IT WHICH ARE LIKE THE LITTLE BRIGHT MOMENTS THAT COME ALONG IN OUR LIVES EVERY NOW AND THEN...

DO YOU FEEL THAT THIS HAS BEEN ONE OF THOSE BRIGHT MOMENTS, CHUCK? DO YOU FEEL THAT THIS HOUR WE HAVE HAD TOGETHER HAS BEEN LIKE A DIAMOND SET IN A BRACELET?

DO YOU FEEL THAT WAY, CHUCK? IF YOU DO, YOU SHOULD TELL ME..

WHY, YES... I THINK YOU'RE RIGHT.. LIFE IS VERY MUCH LIKE A COLLAR..

11-5

NOT A COLLAR, CHUCK.. A BRACELET !!!

SPEAKING OF COLLARS, SWEETIE.. I'M AN EXPERT!

I REMEMBER ONCE BACK ABOUT FIVE YEARS AGO... I SAID THE RIGHT THING..

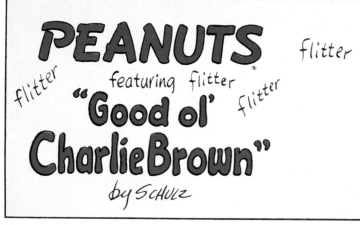

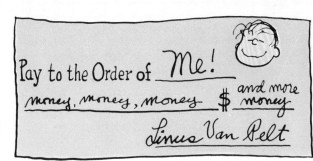

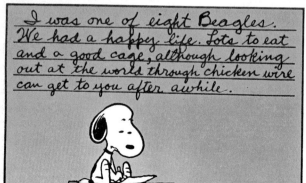

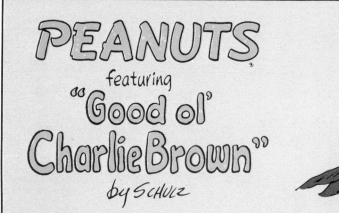

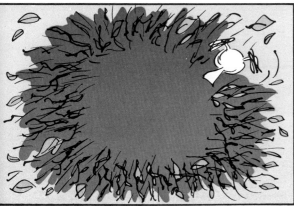

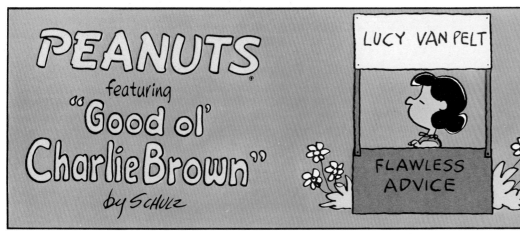

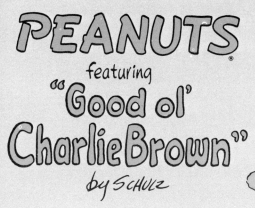

PEANUTS featuring "Good ol' Charlie Brown" by SCHULZ

YES, SIR

IF YOU'RE NOT FEELING WELL, THE VET SAID I SHOULD TAKE YOUR TEMPERATURE, AND THEN CALL HIM BACK...

THAT'S FUNNY... ACCORDING TO THIS, YOUR TEMPERATURE IS ONLY FORTY-TWO...

8-5

..I DON'T UNDERSTAND

SOMEBODY MUST HAVE HAD COLD FEET!

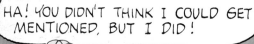

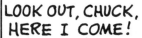

PEANUTS
featuring
"Good ol' CharlieBrown"
by SCHULZ

ZIP!

RAH

rah

11-4

RAH

THINGS LIKE THAT COULD RUIN SPECTATOR SPORTS...

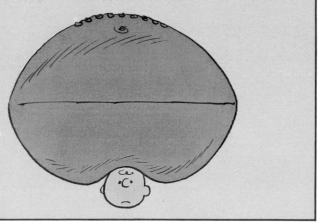

THEY WORK FOR DAYS AHEAD OF TIME, SEE...

AND ON THANKSGIVING DAY THEY ROAST THIS BIRD, SEE, AND THEY...

11-18

KLUNK!

OH, LITTLE FRIEND OF FRIENDS, DON'T WORRY... NO ONE IS GOING TO ROAST YOU!

IF ANYONE TRIED TO ROAST YOU FOR THANKSGIVING, YOU KNOW WHAT I'D DO?

BONK!

I'D PUNCH HIM IN THE NOSE!!

NOW, WHAT BROUGHT THAT ON?

PEANUTS

featuring

"Good ol' Charlie Brown"

by SCHULZ

HERE WE ARE SKATING OUT ONTO WOODSTOCK'S HOME ICE FOR THE BIG HOCKEY GAME...

AND HERE COME THE OFFICIALS...

THE REFEREE

THE LINESMEN

11-25

THE GOAL JUDGES AND THE PENALTY TIMEKEEPER

THE OFFICIAL SCORER AND THE GAME TIMEKEEPER!

WHICH BRINGS UP A SLIGHT PROBLEM...

WHERE DO WE PUT THE ORGAN FOR THE NATIONAL ANTHEM?

SCHULZ

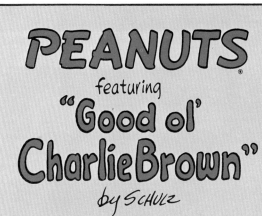

IF HE TRIES TO INSTALL A CABLE CAR AND A SUMMIT RESTAURANT, I'M LEAVING!

3 Surroundings play a definite role in my kind of creativity. I have found from experience that it is best to work in one single place and have a regular routine. The beauty of the surroundings is not necessarily important. In fact, I feel more comfortable in a small, plain room than I do in a fancy studio.

My present studio is a very nice little building near the edge of Santa Rosa, California, and it suits our needs quite well. It may look uncomfortably like doctor's office from the outside, but I shied away from anything that looked too arty or pretentious. We have many people visiting us each week, and we need considerable storage space and a surprising amount of office equipment. When I first started drawing cartoons, it never occurred to me that I would someday need such things as typewriters, a Xerox machine, a postage meter and all different types of stationery, mailing tubes, envelopes and wrapping paper. There are five of us who work at the studio: two secretaries, an accountant, and the president of our firm, which we call Creative Associates. Evelyn Delgado and Pat Lytle are our two secretaries, and Ron Nelson is our accountant who handles all of my financial affairs. Warren Lockhart, the president, spends long hours helping our various licensees to work together and maintaining quality control. It would be very difficult for me to survive without the help of these people.

I have never had anyone work as an assistant on the actual comic strip or comic pages, partly because I feel that there would not be much for them to do. The drawing is relatively simple because of the style I have adopted, and I have too much pride to use anyone else's ideas.

Our day at the studio begins at 9:00 in the morning, but for myself, I find it very hard to get started until the mail has been distributed and I know if there are going to be any special projects for that day. This means that I rarely begin drawing until 9:30 or 10:00. I have also found as the years go by that I am getting to be a very slow starter. It is nice to come to the studio in the morning having at least one idea to draw, but if there is no such idea, then I have to get out my little pad of white paper and begin searching for something. Sometimes ideas come very rapidly but, unfortunately, there are also days when no ideas come at all. If I could know I was going to draw a blank day, then I would go off someplace and do something else. But I always hate to stop trying, so I sit there and make up little conversations with myself, thinking about the past, drawing Snoopy and the others in different poses, hoping something new will come along. There are days when I would like to draw something very philosophical and meaningful, something to touch the hearts of everyone, and find it absolutely impossible. One solution I use at these times is simply to get back to basics. Cartooning is, after all, drawing funny pictures, something a cartoonist should never forget. If a cartoonist remains within his own medium, if he does not let himself become carried too far afield and always remembers that his business is to draw funny pictures, then I believe he will have a minimum of bad days.

It is nice to be surrounded by reference books and be where it is quiet, but being in the same place each day is more important. When I first started drawing Peanuts, I was sharing an apartment with my dad on the second floor across the hall from a dentist's office and above a drugstore and a liquor store. My dad's barbershop was downstairs and around the corner, making it very convenient for him to go to work each day. I used one of the bedrooms of this apartment as my studio and was quite proud of it. When I was first married, we lived with my dad and stepmother for a short time until we could complete preparations for a move to Colorado Springs. During this interlude, I actually drew the comic strip on a card table in the basement of my stepmother's home. In 1951 we moved to Colorado Springs, and I again tried to work at home in one of the bedrooms, but found it difficult to keep up a regular routine. When I couldn't think of any ideas, it was too easy to find some distraction around the house. So I rented a small room in a downtown office building and worked there for almost a year. After we moved back to Minneapolis, I was offered a wonderful little room, which we liked to call the penthouse, at my former employer's, Art Instruction Schools. These were happy days for me. for

I was back with my old friends and in the midst of those invigorating surroundings. Eventually, however, we made another move, this time to California where, once again, I had a solitary place to work. The property we purchased had a studio on it, which had been a photographer's studio, and was all that any cartoonist could ask for. As the years went by and many changes took place among our friends and within our own family, my studio location changed again, and for approximately a year I actually worked in a small room over our ice arena. This became extremely difficult at times, however, for there were simply too many interruptions. We had to have a building completely to ourselves, so we built the structure I work in today.

I am not a very patient person when it comes to drawing pictures, which I have always thought was one of the reasons I became a cartoonist. An illustrator or a painter spends countless hours preparing his canvas, while the cartoonist merely reaches for a sheet of drawing paper. I do very little preliminary sketching and work directly upon the smooth-surfaced pen-and-ink paper, where the final drawing appears. I believe that as little pencil work as possible should go into the drawing, that the cartoonist should draw as much as is practical with the pen itself. I do not believe in the term "inking in." This would be an indication of merely following some prescribed pencil lines, with the inevitable results being less than the original sketch. Once I have thought of an idea,

161

1 Snoopy Place: at the drawing board (left and upper center) ; *a part of the room across from my work area* (upper right) *: and going over the day's mail with Evelyn Delgado . . .*

I can visualize the entire page. Sometimes, if there are as many as ten or twelve panels involved, it is necessary to start with the final panel containing the punch line, and number the panels backward in order to arrange the best spacing. Some ideas also require that the last panel be drawn first to eliminate any doubts as to the effectiveness of that final drawing. It can happen that I think of an idea, then discover that the drawing of that idea is really not practical, or maybe that it cannot be drawn as first visualized. It is far better to discover this by drawing the last panel first than after the entire page has been completed. The last panel in a Sunday comic strip is especially important. When the reader first glances at the Sunday pages of his comics, it is very easy for his eye to drop to the lower right-hand corner and have the whole page spoiled for him. Thus, it is sometimes necessary to try not to attract attention to that panel, to make certain that the beginning panels are interesting enough to keep the reader from skipping to the end. There have been times, for instance, when I wanted to use large lettering in the last panel to emphasize something being said, but decided not to for fear that the reader would be directly attracted to it and see the punch line too soon.

I do not prepare my continuing stories in advance, but usually let the daily episodes take a story where they wish to lead it. I find it is much more important to have a good series of daily ideas than to have a good story line. A comic-strip

with Warren Lockhart, president of Creative Associates, looking over some new licensed products; Pat Lytle who handles the hundreds of requests coming in each day from children around the world (lower left) ; *and Ron Nelson, who takes care of the financial affairs of the company and of the Redwood Empire Ice Arena* (lower right)

These little pencil sketches are made on a small pad of white paper and are probably the best things I do. It is a pity that the freshness is lost when they are translated to the comic page. Many of my most spontaneous ideas come from doodling in this manner, and the doodles themselves produce further ideas that often barely resemble their beginnings. Many times they are simply warm-up sketches on a Monday morning, and sometimes they produce nothing. A person has to start someplace, and I have found that this is my best way.

Bonk!

165

artist should never concentrate so hard on a story line that he allows his daily episodes to become weak. He should never let the reader feel that it is all right if he misses the strip for two or three days because he can pick up the story later on in the week. This is probably one of the worst things a cartoonist can do.

It took several years for me to develop the knack of presenting short stories. I was already using themes and variations, but I believe it was the story of Charlie Brown getting his kite caught in the tree that started me off on these stories. He was so mad that he said he was going to stand beneath the tree, holding on to the string, and not move for the rest of his life. I then had the other characters come up to him, one by one, each day and either say dumb things to him, or something that would prompt him to answer in a sarcastic manner. It was a brief episode, but it did attract some attention and, I believe, new readers. Since then, I have tried to use stories frequently. I find it a good way to think of ideas because once a story gets going, all sorts of little episodes come to mind.

I don't know which story has been my favorite, but one that worked out far beyond my expectations concerned Charlie Brown's problem when, instead of seeing the sun rise early one morning, he saw a huge baseball come up over the horizon. Eventually a rash, similar to the stitching on a baseball, began to appear on his head, and his pediatrician told him it would be a good idea if he went off to camp and got some rest. Be-cause he was embarrassed by the rash, he decided to wear a sack over his head. The first day of camp, all of the boys held a meeting, and someone jokingly nominated the kid with the sack over his head as camp president. Before he knew it, Charlie Brown was running the camp and had the admiration of everyone. It seemed that no matter what he did, it turned out well, and he became known as "Sack" or "Mr. Sack," and became the best-liked and most-admired kid in camp. Unfortunately, he could not resist taking the sack off to see if his rash was cured, and once he had removed the sack, he reverted back to his old self. I don't pretend there is any great truth to this story, or any marvelous moral, but it was a neat little tale and one of which I was proud. Unfortunately, this kind of story does not come along very often, and I am satisfied if I can think of something that good once every year.

The longest series I have ever done involved Peppermint Patty and her ice-skating competition. I was able to stretch it out because it allowed me to go in several directions. First, there was the matter of her having to practice and of her involvement with her ice-skating pro, who was Snoopy. Then there was the making of her skating dress, as she talked little Marcie, against her will, into making the dress for her. I believe this story went on for five weeks and, of course, ended in disaster for poor Peppermint Patty, because the ice-skating competition for which she had prepared so diligently turned out to be a roller-skating competition instead.

166

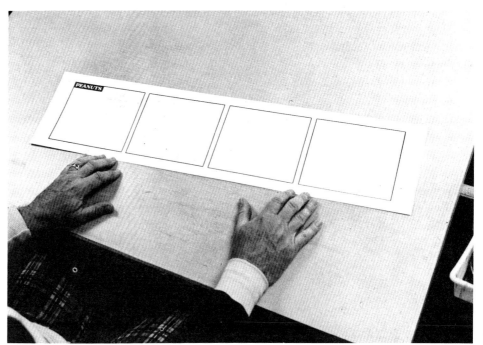

1

THE CREATION OF A STRIP

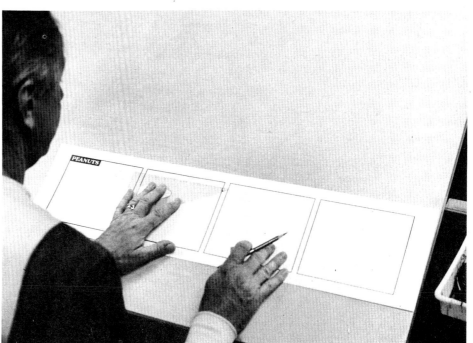

2

3

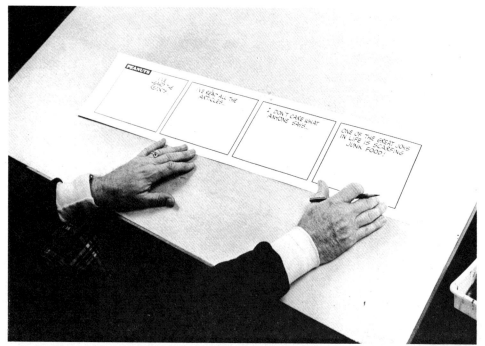

4

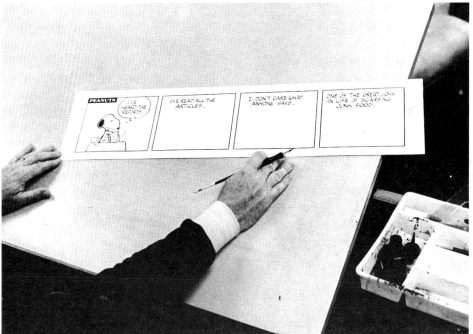

7

8

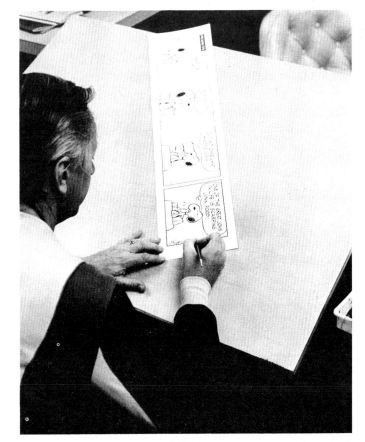

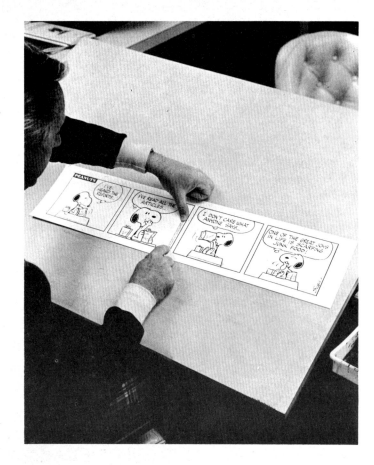

This idea came from a conversation with one of our secretaries about some jelly beans we had sitting on a coffee table in the studio.

The first thing I do is rough out the captions, usually in lettering so ragged that I am the only one who can read it (1). The main purpose is to get the words spaced properly. The next step is to rule in guidelines with a pencil (2). The completed lettering is then done with a C-5 lettering pen. The pose and the expression on the character in the last panel is usually what puts over the idea, so this is frequently sketched in first to make sure that the point will come across. Sometimes I will finish the last panel in ink, but in this case I started with the first panel and worked my way across (3-8).

After the entire strip was completed, I noted that it would be more effective to show some French fried potatoes peeking out of the container, so I went back and added those in the first three panels (9).

When the strip is done, I usually sign it in one of the corners of the last panel (10), then the very important copyright sticker is pasted in an inconspicuous spot (11). All of the pencil lines are erased, and the strip is ready finally to join the group for that week to be mailed to New York.

Pacing is very important, and I usually go back to simple daily episodes after completing a story like this. Having many characters to work with gives you a broad keyboard on which to play, which I believe is important. I think that when you have done a story that gets close to realism, that involves the children themselves doing things that children are likely to do, then it is best, when the story is over, to do something as absurd as Snoopy typing his stories on his little typewriter, sitting atop the doghouse. Here, I am able to take part in a kind of humor that could not be done under regular circumstances. I can have Snoopy type outrageous puns in stories such as the one where he tells of the woman who is afraid to stay home while her husband goes on business trips. "I have solved our problem," the man said, "I have bought you a St. Bernard whose name is Great Reluctance. From now on, when I leave you, I'll be leaving you with Great Reluctance." This is the sort of pun that you would never draw under ordinary circumstances, but it works very well for Snoopy because it falls in with his personality. He has the right combination of innocence and egotism to make it work.

There is sometimes a great temptation to complete one or another of the running themes that are in the feature. It is always tempting to let Charlie Brown kick the football, or to give in and let Schroeder become Lucy's boyfriend. But this is something that has to be avoided. Charlie Brown can never be a winner. He can never win a baseball game because it would destroy the foundation of the strip. We cannot destroy the caricature of his personality any more than we can begin to modify some of his features to make him look more like a real little boy.

Some things happen in the strip simply because I enjoy drawing them. Rain is fun to draw. I pride myself on being able to make nice strokes with the point of the pen, and I also recall how disappointing a rainy day can be to a child. When I think back to those ball games that we looked forward to as teenagers, and how crushed we were if the game had to be postponed because of rain, it brings to mind emotions that can be translated into cartoon ideas.

I don't suppose a person has to be too psychologically observant to notice that boys play a more predominant role in Peanuts than do girls. I have always been self-conscious about this but, after all, I know more about the suffering of little boys growing up than I do the suffering of little girls. I have tried, however, to balance the characters in the strip, but it has only been recently that I have been able to do stories that were predominantly about the girls. I think the best of all was the one concerning ear piercing. Whenever I become involved in a story like this, I do enough research to make it authentic. Phone calls to several different physicians enabled me to find out the problems of having one's ears pierced and to obtain the opinions of doctors as to the advisability of the operation. I was also able to find out the problems of infection, pain, and other such things. It was a successful series, and one that I enjoyed as much as any.

Sunday pages and daily strips pose different problems. When I first began to do Sunday pages, I found the pacing difficult because I seemed to waste too much time getting my episodes started. Gradually, however, I began to see what the problem was and since then have learned to visualize a story or episode as a whole. I then chop off the beginning of that episode to make the action as concentrated as possible. In other words, with no time for the children in the strip to stand around in the first two or three panels, discussing what is going to happen, the action has to begin, in effect, in the middle of the episode, and to proceed rapidly. This would not be as true for a comic feature that involves more realistic characters, but it certainly is true for a strip like mine, which deals in abstract situations.

I have found drawing with pen and ink to be extremely challenging as well as gratifying. I feel that it is possible to achieve something near to what fine artists call "paint quality" when working with the pen. It is unfortunate that newspaper reproduction does not show off some of the good pen-and-ink or brush-and-ink work done by the better artists in our business. The rendering of a comic strip requires a good deal of concentration, and when drawing grass, for instance, I have discovered that I should be "thinking grass."

If I am drawing the boards in a wooden fence, then I should be thinking of the texture of those boards if I am to achieve the appearance of that texture with the pen strokes. We used to have a little pen-and-ink exercise or demonstration that we sent out to the students at the correspondence school. We would draw three sets of pen lines, starting with a very fine set, progressing to a medium set, then ending with a third set of very bold lines. It used to be challenging to see how close we could get those pen lines to each other without having them touch, and to see if we could draw a perfect set. Doing this exercise hundreds of times helped me to develop the pen technique that I now possess. I abandoned the idea of drawing with the brush early in my career, even though I had experimented extensively with it and was reasonably pleased with the results. The characters in Peanuts, however, required a much tighter line.

As the years progressed and my style loosened considerably, the content of the strip, as I have tried to demonstrate, also changed. The important thing is that throughout the development of the strip, style and content have been consistent. I feel very strongly that a cartoonist should not over-caricaturize. The reader must be able to recognize the expressions on the characters' faces, hence, the degree of caricaturization should not be so extreme that various proportions are distorted beyond recognition. Everything should be based on the way things actually look, and the degree of caricaturization should be consistent with the weight of the humor.

People are always concerned with how far in advance a comic strip has to be drawn. Syndicate deadlines vary, of course, but my schedule calls for the Sunday pages to be delivered in New York at least ten weeks ahead of publication date. Anything beyond that is for my own good, and I am constantly trying to lap myself. I try to build up two or three weeks beyond the syndicate deadline to attain a little breathing space. Unfortunately, however, it is a little like running up a glass hill, for no sooner does one arrive almost at the top when he slides rapidly back down to the beginning. It may take me six months to gain a two- or three-week lead, but it seems to take only a few minutes for that lead to disappear.

The most wonderful part of the business is knowing that you are reaching people and communicating with them. This is what makes cartooning such a rewarding profession. In fact, it need not even be done professionally, for a cartoon drawn on such a simple thing as a letter to a friend can be very meaningful.

Lately, letters have been coming in to our studio at the rate of approximately one hundred per day. This varies slightly according to what is going on in the strip or the recent airing of a television show. The last time our valentine show was on

TV, readers responded tremendously to the sad plight of Charlie Brown not receiving any valentines at the school party. One time, I drew an episode where Lucy had made a kite out of Linus's blanket and reported to him that while flying it, the string had broken and that his kite was last seen flying over the trees and off toward the distant horizon. Readers across the country had a lot of fun writing to me, reporting that they had seen it over their hometown or some such place. One vacationing couple reported that they had seen it flying over the Grand Canyon, and several people went along with the whole gag by inserting ads in the want-ad section of their local newspapers, supposedly telling Linus where they had last seen his blanket.

In 1966, during the month of May, I created a series that, fortunately, disturbed quite a few people. I say "fortunately" because, after all, the idea is not only to amuse your readers but to get them so involved with the characters in the strip that they will actually become disturbed if they think something bad is going to happen to any of them. In this case, Linus and Lucy were to move away from the town in which they had been born and raised. No one could quite believe that it was going to happen, and when they finally pulled away in their station wagon, it seemed to be a sad day for everyone involved. Soon the letters and telegrams began to arrive at the studio, and suddenly I realized I had made a mistake, for I had already decided that they would not be gone very long,

that their father would change his mind and bring his family back to their old neighborhood. I wish now that I had had them stay away for at least a couple of months, but I guess I panicked out of fear that I would be seriously criticized by subscribing newspaper editors. At any rate, when I saw how concerned people really were, I knew I had a pretty good thing going. One doctor sent me a telegram that said: HEART-BROKEN OVER CURRENT DEVELOPMENT, BAD FOR PSYCHE OF YOUNG. PLEASE ADVISE. Another telegram said: PLEASE DON'T LET LINUS LEAVE. HE IS LIKE A SON TO ME. I answered that telegram by telling her. "Don't panic. Time heals all wounds." Another very nice girl wrote to me saying that she firmly believed that all 27,000 students at Berkeley were extremely upset. I especially liked the letter from the girl who wrote to say that her mother had a very insecure feeling about the whole situation and that if Linus and Lucy did not return to their old neighborhood, their whole family was going to crack-up. One young bible-college student from Oklahoma sent me a letter on which he had written in very huge letters the scream that I use in the strip so often—AAAUGH—and at the bottom he added the P.S.: "How many more sleepless nights must I spend wondering the fate of Linus and Lucy??—Help!" I also liked the postcard from Redwood City, California, which said, "Fear has gripped me at the breakfast table the last couple of mornings. I can't leave for work without knowing what is going to happen to Linus and Lucy." A girl from Stockton wrote, and after expressing her worry about the children she added the word "Sob," repeating it a hundred times at the bottom of the letter. Another very nice woman from Dayton, Ohio, asked me on a postcard in a most plaintive manner, "Why, why have you done this?" and then signed it, "In reverence for the departed." When the series ended, and Linus and Lucy had finally come back to their original neighborhood, several papers made it a front-page story and expressed their relief that the two characters were home. I received one particularly interesting letter from a woman who said, "Today, here in our household in Georgia, you have restored security and a sense of well-being."

I am not always prepared for some of the reactions that certain strips have brought. In 1970, Linus asked Lucy, "What would happen if there were a beautiful and highly intelligent child up in Heaven waiting to be born, and his parents decided that the two children they already had were enough?" Lucy replied, "Your ignorance of theology and medicine is appalling." In the last panel Linus said, "Well, I still think it is a good question." I was astounded when letters began to pour in on both sides of a subject that I had not realized I had touched. It was not my intention to get involved in a contraception or abortion debate. My point was simply that people all too frequently discuss things that they know little about. For the next several weeks I received letters complimenting me on my stand on population control, while I also received letters from readers who were fighting abortion. Both sides were sometimes complimentary, sometimes critical.

Another Sunday page that stirred up far more trouble than I had anticipated showed Sally coming home and saying to her brother, Charlie Brown, that she had something to tell him but, evidently, did not want anyone else to hear. They went off by themselves and hid behind the couch in their living room where Sally whispered very quietly, "We prayed in school today." I have letters from people who told me that this was one of the most disgusting things they had seen in a comic strip, that they did not think it was funny and indeed thought it was extremely sacrilegious. Another woman, writing from West Orange, New Jersey said she thought the page should be hung in the Hall of Fame, adding, "I think it is beautiful, and you have our heartiest support." This page, like the other, upset people on both sides of the subject, and also pleased people on both sides. Oddly enough, requests began to pour into United Feature Syndicate in New York to use reprints of the page to promote both the fight to reestablish prayer in school, and the fight to eliminate prayer in school. The simplest solution was to deny everyone the right to reprint the strip.

In all the years I have been drawing Peanuts, I believe I have upset no other professional group more than optometrists. This is because every time any of the children in Peanuts have an eye problem, they always visit an ophthalmologist. The reason for this is that I have several friends who are ophthalmologists, and they have acquainted me with the nature of childhood eye problems. In 1966 I drew a series of episodes that showed Sally going to her ophthalmologist and having one of her eyes patched because "lazy eye" had been diagnosed. I immediately received angry letters from optometrists who said that she could just as well have gone to one of them as to an ophthalmologist. My research disagrees with them. However, they are still convinced that it was all a plot to discredit their profession, which, of course, is not true at all. I was concerned only for the children.

It is extremely important for a cartoonist to be a person of observation. He not only has to observe the strange things that people do and listen to the strange things that they say, but he also has to be reasonably observant as to the appearance of objects in the world around him. Some cartoonists keep a thorough file of things they might have to draw, such as a child's tricycle, or perhaps some kind of farming equipment. Other cartoonists do a good deal of actual sketching. This kind of observing has led me to something I can only describe as mental drawing, and at times that has become a real burden, for I seem to be unable to stop it. While I am carrying on a conversation with someone, I find that I am drawing with my eyes. I find myself observing how his shirt collar comes around from behind his neck and perhaps casts a slight shadow on one side. I observe how the wrinkles in his sleeve form and how his arm may be resting on the edge of the chair. I observe how the features on his face move back and forth in perspective as he rotates his head. It actually is a form of sketching and I believe that it is the next best thing to drawing itself. But I sometimes feel it is obsessive, like people who click their teeth and find that they have to do it in even numbers, or people who cannot resist counting telephone poles. It may even be some kind of neurosis, but at least it accomplishes something for me.

If you should ask me why I have been successful with Peanuts, I would have to admit that being highly competitive has played a strong role. I am not one who will rage uncontrollably when losing at something, but I must admit that I would rather win than lose. In the thing that I do best, which is drawing a comic strip, it is important to me that I win. Each cartoonist fights for attention on the comic page. Some get it easily by being given more space than others, and some try to attract attention by using thick black borders around their panels, while some try for attention by using dramatic areas of solid black in their drawings. I was forced to present a strip that was the tiniest on the page, so I had to fight back by using white space. On a page jammed with comic strips, a small feature with lots of white space attracted attention. Once you get the attention, of course, you must retain it with the quality

SNOOPY and the RED BARON

Snoopy's imaginary combat career as a World War I flying ace has brought in a wide variety of mail. I have had veterans from that war write to me, wondering if perhaps I had been part of their outfit. And I have had others send me photographs of places where Snoopy has flown, such as this one of Pont-à-Mousson. I have frequently made use of this kind of material to authenticate Snoopy's adventures.

*Amy and I rode with this big stuffed Snoopy in the Grand
Marshal's car during the 1974 Tournament of Roses
Parade. On that day a strip appeared—drawn, of course,
six weeks ahead of time—which made the only personal
reference I have ever used in the strip. I believe the original
is on permanent exhibition at parade headquarters in
Pasadena. I was invited to be Grand Marshal by
Ed Wilson, that year's parade president, and it was
a tremendous experience.*

of your ideas, but that is your own responsibility. I hope that I am not the kind who grows bitter as the years take the inevitable toll on my career. I do know for sure that I work very hard to make my comic strip the very best one on that newspaper page each day. Whether or not I succeed is immaterial. I know that I really try. You could almost say that I view the comic page as a golf tournament or a tennis match, and it is important for me to be in the finals.

I still enjoy going to work each day, though friends who know me well can testify to the fact that I never actually use the term "work." If I have to say that I will not be free to do something on a certain day, I will always put it: "I have to go to the studio and draw funny pictures." It could be a superstition, but I guess it is really that I don't want anyone to think that what I do is that much work. It is one of the few situations in my life where I feel totally secure. When I sit behind the drawing board I feel that I am in command. I am comfortable in my studio and I am reasonably proud of many of the things that I have drawn. I think that I have done my share toward contibuting to the advancement of our profession and this also makes me proud. There have been a few regrets, of course. I think the fact that the Peanuts strip has always been printed so small (the size of the feature was developed to overcome sales resistance during a time of newsprint shortage) has contributed toward a dangerous and

negative trend. Most comic features begin with just a daily run, and if that feature is successful the artist is rewarded with a Sunday page. There is a real struggle for the limited space that is available in the Sunday section of the average newspaper. Years ago, each feature covered an entire page of the newspaper. This space has shrunk, however, to half pages, one-third pages, and now quarter pages. This has made a mockery out of many otherwise fine features. It is like putting Cinerama on a ten-inch television screen. And just as I have resented the size that I have been forced to work in, I have resented the title "Peanuts" that was forced upon me. I still am convinced that it is the worst title ever thought of for a comic strip.

We have covered the world with licensed products—everything from sweatshirts to lunchboxes to toothbrushes—and have been criticized many times for this, although for reasons that I cannot accept. My best answer to such critics is always that the feature itself has not suffered because of our extracurricular activities. I have drawn every one of the 10,000 strips that have appeared and I have thought of every idea. Not once did I ever let our other activities interfere with our main product—the comic strip. Our most severe criticism came when we took on the advertising account for the Ford Motor Company. For some reason many people thought this was too much, but I believe that the ads we turned out were of high quality and were dignified. Our television work has always received my closest attention, and we have even tried to watch carefully to see that we had sponsors who would retain the dignity of the feature. It has always been a mystery to me how we can be accused of overcommercializing something that is basically a commercial product.

But it really does not matter what you are called, or where your work is placed, as long as it brings some kind of joy to some person someplace. To create something out of nothing is a wonderful experience. To take a blank piece of paper and draw characters that people love and worry about is extremely satisfying. I hope very much that I will be allowed to do it for another twenty-five years.

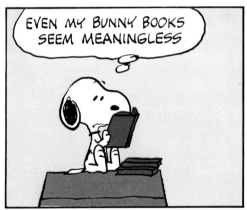

PEANUTS featuring "Good ol' Charlie Brown" by Schulz

Madam Fullcharge

I'M READY!

SO IT'S "SHOW AND TELL" TIME AGAIN, IS IT? WELL, DO I EVER HAVE A SURPRISE FOR YOU TODAY!

I HAVE A LITTLE FILM TO SHOW YOU THAT'S GONNA KNOCK YOUR EYES OUT!

1-20

NO, MA'AM... THAT'S ONLY AN EXPRESSION..

ALL RIGHT, IF I CAN HAVE A COUPLE OF YOU STRONG TYPES LIFT THIS PROJECTOR INTO PLACE, WE CAN GET THIS SHOW ON THE ROAD!

NO, LET'S PUT IT ON THAT TABLE BACK THERE... HOW ABOUT YOU FOUR WEIRDOS MOVING THAT TABLE?

AND I'LL NEED A COUPLE MORE TO PUT THIS SCREEN UP... LET'S GO!! ON THE DOUBLE, THERE!

STRETCH THAT CORD ACROSS THE BACK, AND PLUG IT INTO THAT SOCKET IN THE CORNER...

OKAY, SOMEONE RUN DOWN TO THE CUSTODIAN THEN, AND GET AN EXTENSION! YOU THERE, GET GOING!!

NOW, WHAT ABOUT THOSE WINDOW SHADES? LET'S HAVE ALL OF YOU WHO SIT ALONG THE SIDE THERE PULL DOWN THOSE STUPID SHADES..

AND I'LL NEED SOMEONE ON THE LIGHT SWITCH... ONE VOLUNTEER... YOU THERE, HONEY, GET THE SWITCH!

IS THAT THE BELL ALREADY?

OKAY, WE'LL TAKE IT TOMORROW FROM HERE.. EVERYONE BE IN PLACE BY NINE! THANK YOU, AND GOOD MORNING!

Schulz

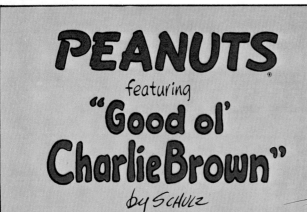

PEANUTS
featuring
"Good ol' Charlie Brown"
by Schulz

SOMETIMES I THINK YOU DON'T REALIZE THAT YOU COULD LOSE ME...

ARE YOU SURE YOU WANT TO SUFFER THE TORTURES OF THE MEMORY OF A LOST LOVE?

DO YOU KNOW THE TORTURES OF THE MEMORY OF A LOST LOVE?

IT'S AWFUL!!!

2-24

IT WILL HAUNT YOU NIGHT AND DAY!!

YOU'LL WAKE UP AT NIGHT SCREAMING!

YOU CAN'T EAT! YOU CAN'T SLEEP!! YOU'LL WANT TO SMASH THINGS!

YOU'LL HATE YOURSELF AND THE WORLD AND EVERYBODY IN IT!

OOOOOO!!!

ARE YOU SURE YOU WANT TO RISK LOSING ME?

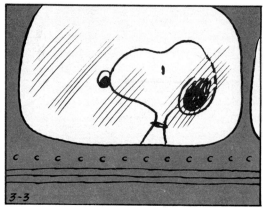

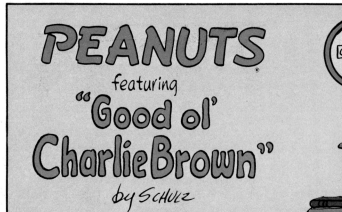

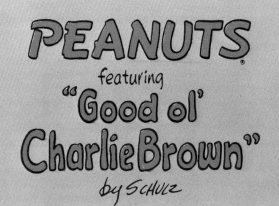

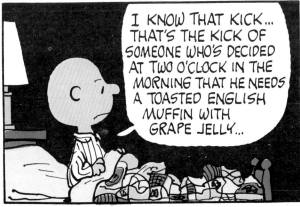

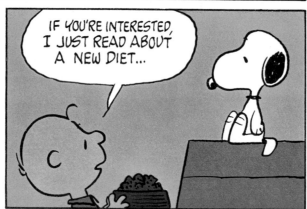

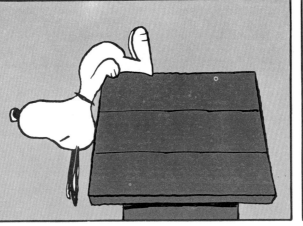

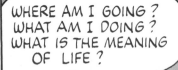

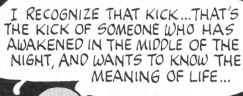

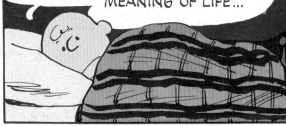

A Peanuts Chronology

Peanuts Bibliography

A PEANUTS CHRONOLOGY

1950

October 2: Peanuts strip begins with Charlie Brown, Snoopy, Shermy, and Patty

1951

Schroeder is introduced

1952

January 6: First Peanuts Sunday page   *First Peanuts book collection published by Rinehart*
Lucy makes her first appearance   *Linus enters strip*

1955

Charles Schulz awarded National Cartoonists Society "Reuben"

1958

Humorist of the Year Award from Yale

1959

 1959

Sally enters strip

1960

School Bell Award from National Education Society

1961

Frieda introduced into strip

1962

Happiness Is a Warm Puppy *published by Determined Publications*
Best Humor Strip of the Year Award from National Cartoonists Society

1963

Honorary degree from Anderson College, Anderson, Indiana

1964

The Gospel According to Peanuts *by Robert Short published by John Knox Press*
Second "Reuben" awarded Charles Schulz by National Cartoonists Society

 # 1965

April 9: Peanuts appears on cover of Time *magazine*

Television special "A Charlie Brown Christmas" wins Emmy Award and Peabody Award

October 10: Snoopy appears in first Red Baron sequence

1966

Snoopy's doghouse burns—he receives many letters of condolence   *Television special "Charlie Brown's All-Stars"*
June 11: Honorary Doctor of Humane Letters from St. Mary's College, California

1967

Certificate of Merit: Art Director's Club of New York
March 17: Snoopy and Charlie Brown make the cover of Life   *Television special "You're in Love, Charlie Brown"*
May 24: Charles Schulz Day, proclaimed by Governor Reagan of California
The play You're a Good Man, Charlie Brown *opens off-Broadway*
and eventually becomes the most-produced musical in the history of the American theater

1968

Snoopy joins Manned Flight Awareness Program   *Franklin enters strip* *Redwood Empire Ice Arena opens*

1969

Snoopy and Charlie Brown accompany astronauts into space   *April 12: Lucy and Snoopy make the cover of* Saturday Review
Full-length feature film A Boy Named Charlie Brown *(a Lee Mendelson—Bill Melendez Production)*
Television documentary "Charlie Brown and Charlie Schulz" (written by Lee Mendelson)

1970

Woodstock introduced into strip   *Snoopy joins the* Ice Follies

1971

June 17: Peanuts Day in San Diego—Charles Schulz given key to the city

Marcie enters strip   Snoopy publishes It Was a Dark and Stormy Night (Holt, Rinehart and Winston)

Snoopy joins Johnny Horizon Environmental Program

December 27: Snoopy, Charlie Brown, Linus, Lucy, and Woodstock make cover of NewsweekSnoopy joins Holiday on Ice

Ice Follies television show—"Snoopy's International Ice Follies"

1972

Second full-length feature film Snoopy, Come Home (a Lee Mendelson—Bill Melendez Production)

Rerun introduced into strip

1973

You're a Good Man, Charlie Brown shown on "Hallmark Hall of Fame"

Charles Schulz given Big Brother of the Year Award in San Francisco

U.S. Government uses Snoopy as Energy Conservation Symbol

1974

Charles Schulz Grand Marshal of Tournament of Roses Parade, Pasadena

Television special "A Charlie Brown Thanksgiving" earns an Emmy Award for

Charles Schulz as writer of the show (a Lee Mendelson—Bill Melendez Production)

216

PEANUTS BIBLIOGRAPHY

The comic strip Peanuts appears in 1,655 newspapers and magazines around the world, including 1,480 in North America.
All titles cited in this bibliography are collections of daily and/or Sunday strips, with the following exceptions:

one asterisk (*) denotes a book version of a television program (story by Charles Schulz, production by Lee Mendelson and Bill Melendez)

two asterisks (**) denotes a book version of a feature motion picture (story by Charles Schulz, production by Lee Mendelson and Bill Melendez)

one dagger (†) denotes a storybook with special drawings and text by Charles Schulz

two daggers (††) denotes a book that makes special use of individual panels or characters from the strip

1952

Peanuts. New York: Rinehart (currently Holt, Rinehart and Winston).

1954

More Peanuts. New York: Rinehart (currently Holt, Rinehart and Winston).

1956

Good Grief, More Peanuts! New York: Rinehart (currently Holt, Rinehart and Winston).

1957

Good Ol' Charlie Brown. New York: Rinehart (currently Holt, Rinehart and Winston).

1958

Snoopy. New York: Rinehart (currently Holt, Rinehart and Winston).

1959

You're Out of Your Mind, Charlie Brown! New York: Rinehart (currently Holt, Rinehart and Winston).

But We Love You, Charlie Brown. New York: Rinehart (currently Holt, Rinehart and Winston).

Peanuts Revisited. New York: Rinehart (currently Holt, Rinehart and Winston).

1960

Go Fly a Kite, Charlie Brown. New York: Holt, Rinehart and Winston.

Radiserne 1. Copenhagen: Gyldendal.

1961

Peanuts Every Sunday. New York: Holt, Rinehart and Winston.

Radiserne 2. Copenhagen: Gyldendal.

Søndags-Radiserne 1. Copenhagen: Gyldendal.

1962

It's a Dog's Life, Charlie Brown. New York: Holt, Rinehart and Winston.

You Can't Win, Charlie Brown. New York: Holt, Rinehart and Winston.

††*Happiness Is a Warm Puppy.* San Francisco: Determined.

The Wonderful World of Peanuts (selected Vol. 1 from *More Peanuts*). New York: Fawcett.

Hey, Peanuts! (selected Vol. 2 from *More Peanuts*). New York: Fawcett.

Radiserne 3. Copenhagen: Gyldendal.

Søndags-Radiserne 2. Copenhagen: Gyldendal.

1963

Snoopy, Come Home. New York: Holt, Rinehart and Winston.

You Can Do It, Charlie Brown. New York: Holt, Rinehart and Winston.

††*Security Is a Thumb and a Blanket.* San Francisco: Determined.

Good Grief, Charlie Brown! (selected Vol. 1 from *Good Grief, More Peanuts!*). New York: Fawcett.

For the Love of Peanuts! (selected Vol. 2 from

Good Grief, More Peanuts!). New York: Fawcett.

Fun with Peanuts (selected Vol. 1 from *Good Ol' Charlie Brown*). New York: Fawcett.

Skratta med Snobben. Stockholm: Ahlen & Akerlunds.

Arriva Charlie Brown! Milan: Milano Libri Edizione.

Radiserne 4. Copenhagen: Gyldendal.

Søndags-Radiserne 3. Copenhagen: Gyldendal.

1964

We're Right Behind You, Charlie Brown. New York: Holt, Rinehart and Winston.

As You Like It, Charlie Brown. New York: Holt, Rinehart and Winston.

††*I Need All the Friends I Can Get.* San Francisco: Determined.

††*Christmas Is Together Time.* San Francisco: Determined.

Here Comes Charlie Brown (selected Vol. 2

from *Good Ol' Charlie Brown*). New York: Fawcett.

Povero Charlie Brown! Milan: Milano Libri Edizione.

Il Terzo Libro di Charlie Brown. Milan: Milano Libri Edizione.

Radiserne 5. Copenhagen: Gyldendal.

Søndags-Radiserne 4. Copenhagen: Gyldendal.

1965

Sunday's Fun Day, Charlie Brown. New York: Holt, Rinehart and Winston.

*A Charlie Brown Christmas. New York: World.

††*Love Is Walking Hand in Hand.* San Francisco: Determined.

Very Funny, Charlie Brown (selected Vol. 1 from *You're Out of Your Mind, Charlie Brown!*). New York: Fawcett.

What Next, Charlie Brown (selected Vol. 2 from *You're Out of Your Mind, Charlie Brown!*). New York: Fawcett.

Bonjour, Peanuts! Marcinelle-Charleroi: Dupuis.

Peanuts à Vendre. Marcinelle-Charleroi: Dupuis.

L'Aquilone e Charlie Brown. Milan: Milano Libri Edizione.

Radiserne 6. Copenhagen: Gyldendal.

Søndags-Radiserne 5. Copenhagen: Gyldendal.

1966

You Need Help, Charlie Brown. New York: Holt, Rinehart and Winston.

†*Snoopy and the Red Baron.* New York: Holt, Rinehart and Winston.

*Charlie Brown's All-Stars. New York: World.

*It's the Great Pumpkin, Charlie Brown. New York: World.

††*Home Is on Top of a Dog House.* San Francisco: Determined.

We're on Your Side, Charlie Brown (selected Vol. 1 from *But We Love You, Charlie Brown*). New York: Fawcett.

You Are Too Much, Charlie Brown (selected Vol. 2 from *But We Love You, Charlie Brown*). New York: Fawcett.

Here Comes Snoopy (selected Vol. 1 from *Snoopy*). New York: Fawcett.

You're a Winner, Charlie Brown (selected Vol.1 from *Go Fly a Kite, Charlie Brown*). New York: Fawcett.

Hardi, Peanuts! Marcinelle-Charleroi: Dupuis.

Vita da Cani, Charlie Brown. Milan: Milano Libri Edizione.

E Domenica, Charlie Brown! Milan: Milano Libri Edizione.

Un Natale di Charlie Brown. Milan: Casa Editrice Valentino Bompiani.

Radiserne 7. Copenhagen: Gyldendal.

Søndags-Radiserne 6. Copenhagen: Gyldendal.

1967

The Unsinkable Charlie Brown. New York: Holt, Rinehart and Winston.

You'll Flip, Charlie Brown. New York: Holt, Rinehart and Winston.

*You're in Love, Charlie Brown. New York: World.

††*Happiness Is a Sad Song.* San Francisco: Determined.

Let's Face It, Charlie Brown (selected Vol. 2 from *Go Fly a Kite, Charlie Brown*). New York: Fawcett.

Good Ol' Snoopy (selected Vol. 2 from *Snoopy*). New York: Fawcett.

For Love of Peanuts! London: Hodder Fawcett.

You're a Winner, Charlie Brown. London: Hodder Fawcett.

*Snobben, Karl och Julen. Stockholm: Tidens Förlag.

Snobben. Stockholm: Bokförlaget Herthel.

†*Snoopy und der Rote Baron.* Rienbek: Carlsen Verlag.

†*Snoopy e il Barone Rosso.* Milan: Milano Libri Edizione.

Niente da Fare, Charlie Brown! Milan: Milano Libri Edizione.

Coraggio, Charlie Brown! Milan: Milano Libri Edizione.

La Squadra di Charlie Brown. Milan: Milano Libri Edizione.

Radiserne 8. Copenhagen: Gyldendal.

Søndags-Radiserne 7. Copenhagen: Gyldendal.

1968

You're Something Else, Charlie Brown. New York: Holt, Rinehart and Winston.

Peanuts Treasury. New York: Holt, Rinehart and Winston.

You're You, Charlie Brown. New York: Holt, Rinehart and Winston.

*He's Your Dog, Charlie Brown. New York: World.

††*Suppertime.* San Francisco: Determined.

††*Peanuts Cook Book.* San Francisco: Determined.

Who Do You Think You Are, Charlie Brown (selected Vol. 1 from *Peanuts Every Sunday*). New York: Fawcett.

You're My Hero, Charlie Brown (selected Vol. 2 from *Peanuts Every Sunday*). New York: Fawcett.

This Is Your Life, Charlie Brown (selected Vol. 1 from *It's a Dog's Life, Charlie Brown*). New York: Fawcett.

Slide, Charlie Brown, Slide! (selected Vol. 2 from *It's a Dog's Life, Charlie Brown*). New York: Fawcett.

Fun with Peanuts. London: Hodder Fawcett.

Good Old Snoopy. London: Hodder Fawcett.

Here Comes Snoopy. London: Hodder Fawcett.

Let's Face It, Charlie Brown. London: Hodder Fawcett.

This Is Your Life, Charlie Brown. London: Hodder Fawcett.

Who Do You Think You Are, Charlie Brown. London: Hodder Fawcett.

You're My Hero, Charlie Brown. London: Hodder Fawcett.

†*Snobben och Röde Baronen.* Stockholm: Tidens Förlag.

*Snobben, Linus och Pumpagubben. Stockholm: Tidens Förlag.

Snobbens Karl och Brevvännen. Copenhagen: Carlsen Verlag.

Usch små Systrar. Copenhagen: Carlsen Verlag.

Sol och Sommar och Linus. Copenhagen: Carlsen Verlag.

Linus och Hans Fröken. Copenhagen : Carlsen Verlag.

Doktor Gullan. Copenhagen : Carlsen Verlag.

Snobbar är vi Allihopa. Copenhagen : Carlsen Verlag.

Snobben. Stockholm : Bokförlaget Herthel.

Snobben Karl och Linus. Stockholm : Bokförlaget Herthel.

Vilken Lycka Snobben. Stockholm : Bokförlaget Herthel.

Jag Älskar Dig Snobben. Stockholm : Bokförlaget Herthel.

Du Är Min Hund Snobben. Stockholm : Bokförlaget Herthel.

Ala Jannita, Jaska Jokunen. Helsinki : Sanoma Oy.

Com Vulguis, Charlie Brown. Barcelona : Edicions 62.

Knøttene. Oslo : Chr. Schibsteds Forlag.

Charlie Brown und Snoopy. Stuttgart and Zurich : Delphin Verlag.

Du bist verliebt, Charlie Brown. Stuttgart and Zurich : Delphin Verlag.

Das war ein kurzer Sommer, Charlie Brown. Stuttgart and Zurich : Delphin Verlag.

Siamo con Te, Charlie Brown! Milan : Milano Libri Edizione.

Come Ti Pare, Charlie Brown. Milan : Milano Libri Edizione.

Snoopy. Milan : Milano Libri Edizione.

Il Bambino a una Dimensione. Milan : Arnoldo Mondadori Editore.

Radiserne 9. Copenhagen : Gyldendal.

Søndags-Radiserne 8. Copenhagen : Gyldendal.

1969

Snoopy, Vuelve a Casa. New York : Holt, Rinehart and Winston.

Reviens, Snoopy. New York : Holt, Rinehart and Winston.

Vas-y, Charlie Brown. New York : Holt, Rinehart and Winston.

Adelante, Charlie Brown. New York : Holt, Rinehart and Winston.

**A Boy Named Charlie Brown.* New York : Holt, Rinehart and Winston.

You've Had It, Charlie Brown. New York : Holt, Rinehart and Winston.

†*Snoopy and His Sopwith Camel.* New York : Holt, Rinehart and Winston.

Charlie Brown and Charles Schulz (with Lee Mendelson). New York : World.

**It Was a Short Summer, Charlie Brown.* New York : World.

All This and Snoopy, Too (selected Vol. 1 from *You Can't Win, Charlie Brown*). New York : Fawcett.

Here's to You, Charlie Brown (selected Vol. 2 from *You Can't Win, Charlie Brown*). New York : Fawcett.

Nobody's Perfect, Charlie Brown (selected Vol. 1 from *You Can Do It, Charlie Brown*). New York : Fawcett.

You're a Brave Man, Charlie Brown (selected Vol. 2 from *You Can Do It, Charlie Brown*). New York : Fawcett.

†*Snoopy and the Red Baron.* New York : Fawcett.

All This and Snoopy, Too. London : Hodder Fawcett.

Good Grief, Charlie Brown! London : Hodder Fawcett.

Here's to You, Charlie Brown. London : Hodder Fawcett.

Nobody's Perfect, Charlie Brown. London : Hodder Fawcett.

Slide, Charlie Brown, Slide! London : Hodder Fawcett.

Very Funny, Charlie Brown. London : Hodder Fawcett.

We're on Your Side, Charlie Brown. London : Hodder Fawcett.

Meet the Peanuts Gang. London : Knight Books.

**Snobben, Karl och Kärleken.* Stockholm : Tidens Förlag.

Jag Gillar Dig Snobben. Stockholm : Bokförlaget Herthel.

Milda Makter Snobben. Stockholm : Bokförlaget Herthel.

**Jaska Jokusen Joulu.* Helsinki : Sanoma Oy.

†*Ressu Ja Punainen Paroni.* Helsinki : Sanoma Oy.

Paiva Paistaa, Jaska Jokunen. Helsinki : Sanoma Oy.

Olet Sopo, Jaska Jokunen. Helsinki : Sanoma Oy.

Ressu Eduskuntaan. Helsinki : Sanoma Oy.

Snoopy, el Gos Unidimensional. Barcelona : Edicions 62.

†*Sniff og Den Røde Baron.* Oslo : Chr. Schibsteds Forlag.

Knøttene Kommer Igjen. Oslo : Chr. Schibsteds Forlag.

Lørdagsknøttene. Oslo : Chr. Schibsteds Forlag.

Schröder—Oder : Beethoven, Du bist der Grösste! Götzenhain : Aar Verlag.

Linus—Oder : Wo ist meine Schmusedecke? Götzenhain : Aar Verlag.

Hallo, Snoopy! Götzenhain : Aar Verlag.

Snoopy auf dem Mond. Götzenhain : Aar Verlag.

Zieh Leine, Charlie Braun! Götzenhain : Aar Verlag.

Luzie—Oder : Wer mag seine grosse Schwester? Götzenhain : Aar Verlag.

Akkanbe! Charlie Brown. Tokyo : Tsurushobo Publications Limited.

Shobokure Charlie Brown. Tokyo : Tsurushobo Publications Limited.

Gu-gu-gu Snoopy. Tokyo : Tsurushobo Publications Limited.

Snoopy Ontaishoo. Tokyo : Tsurushobo Publications Limited.

Gottsun Linus. Tokyo : Tsurushobo Publications Limited.

Mooretsu Lucy. Tokyo : Tsurushobo Publications Limited.

Zukkoke Snoopy. Tokyo : Tsurushobo Publications Limited.

Kodokune Charlie Brown. Tokyo : Tsurushobo Publications Limited.

Shikkarishiteyo Charlie Brown. Tokyo : Tsurushobo Publications Limited.

Ikasuwa Charlie Brown. Tokyo : Tsurushobo Publications Limited.

Iziwaru Lucy. Tokyo : Tsurushobo Publications Limited.

Oshaburi Linus. Tokyo : Tsurushobo Publications Limited.

C'era una Volta, Charlie Brown. Milan : Milano Libri Edizione.

Doctor Linus. Milan : Milano Libri Edizione.

Radisebogen. Copenhagen : Gyldendal.

Radiserne 10. Copenhagen : Gyldendal.

Søndags-Radiserne 9. Copenhagen : Gyldendal.

*Radisebogen Du er Forelsket, Søren Brun. Copenhagen : Gyldendal.

†Nuser og den Røde Baron. Copenhagen : Illustrationsforlaget.

1970

Hay Que Ayudarte, Charlie Brown. New York : Holt, Rinehart and Winston.

Ça Ne Va Pas, Charlie Brown. New York : Holt, Rinehart and Winston.

Peanuts Classics. New York : Holt, Rinehart and Winston.

You're Out of Sight, Charlie Brown. New York : Holt, Rinehart and Winston.

††Peanuts Lunch Bag Cook Book. San Francisco : Determined.

We Love You, Snoopy (selected from *Snoopy, Come Home*). New York : Fawcett.

Peanuts for Everybody (selected Vol. 1 from *We're Right Behind You, Charlie Brown*). New York : Fawcett.

You've Done It Again, Charlie Brown (selected Vol. 2 from *We're Right Behind You, Charlie Brown*). New York : Fawcett.

Charlie Brown and Snoopy (selected Vol. 1 from *As You Like It, Charlie Brown*). New York : Fawcett.

Here Comes Charlie Brown. London : Hodder Fawcett.

Hey, Peanuts! London : Hodder Fawcett.

Peanuts for Everybody. London : Hodder Fawcett.

We Love You, Snoopy. London : Hodder Fawcett.

You Are Too Much, Charlie Brown. London : Hodder Fawcett.

You're a Brave Man, Charlie Brown. London : Hodder Fawcett.

Don't Tread on Charlie Brown. London : Knight Books.

**A Boy Named Charlie Brown. London : Knight Books.

*Men Snobben, Vad Tar du Dig Till? Stockholm : Tidens Förlag.

**Snobben, Karl & Co. Stockholm : Tidens Förlag.

Alla Tiders Snobben. Stockholm : Bokförlaget Herthel.

En Gång Till Snobben. Stockholm : Bokförlaget Herthel.

Min Vän Snobben. Stockholm : Bokförlaget Herthel.

Snobben och Hans Värld. 3 vols. Stockholm : Bokförlaget Herthel.

*Se no Rakkautta, Jaska Jokunen. Helsinki : Sanoma Oy.

**Eläköön, Jaska Jokunen. Helsinki : Sanoma Oy.

Plit Seis, Jaska Jokunen. Helsinki : Sanoma Oy.

Charlie Braun und Seine Freunde. Ravensburg : Otto Maier Verlag.

Schröder—Oder : Happy Birthday, Lieber Beethoven! Götzenhain : Aar Verlag.

Snoopy und die Peanuts-Knirpse. Götzenhain : Aar Verlag.

Bleib am Ball, Charlie Braun! Götzenhain : Aar Verlag.

Doktor Luzie. Götzenhain : Aar Verlag.

Lebenskünstler Snoopy. Götzenhain : Aar Verlag.

Immer wieder Peanuts. Götzenhain : Aar Verlag.

Lieber Brieffreund. Reinbek : Carlsen Verlag.

Liebes Fräulein Othmar. Reinbek : Carlsen Verlag.

Tom hat Heimweh. Reinbek : Carlsen Verlag.

Diese kleinen Brüder. Reinbek : Carlsen Verlag.

Liebes kleines rothaariges Mädchen. Reinbek : Carlsen Verlag.

*Knøttenes Julebok. Oslo : Chr. Schibsteds Forlag.

Bom for Baltus. Oslo : Chr. Schibsteds Forlag.

Knøttene for full fart. Oslo : Chr. Schibsteds Forlag.

Een Maaltje Charlie Met Snoopy Toe. Utrecht/Antwerp : A.W. Bruna & Zoon.

Niemand Is Volmaakt, Charlie Brown. Utrecht/Antwerp : A.W. Bruna & Zoon.

Wat Je Ook Doet, Charlie Brown. Utrecht/Antwerp : A. W. Bruna & Zoon.

Kop Op, Charlie Brown. Utrecht/Antwerp : A.W. Bruna & Zoon.

Zero Zero Snoopy. Tokyo : Tsurushobo Publications Limited.

Usunoro Charlie Brown. Tokyo : Tsurushobo Publications Limited.

Konnichiwa Charlie Brown. Tokyo : Tsurushobo Publications Limited.

Gebbakko Lucy. Tokyo : Tsurushobo Publications Limited.

Yattaze Linus. Tokyo : Tsurushobo Publications Limited.

Chakkari Snoopy. Tokyo : Tsurushobo Publications Limited.

Sabishigariyano Charlie Brown. Tokyo : Tsurushobo Publications Limited.

Go! Go! Snoopy. Tokyo : Tsurushobo Publications Limited.

Ohayoo Linus. Tokyo : Tsurushobo Publications Limited.

Harenchi! Snoopy. Tokyo : Tsurushobo Publications Limited.

Charlie Brown no Kakkoii Eikaiwa Gakko. Tokyo : Tsurushobo Publications Limited.

Snoopy no Zukkoke Eikaiwa Gakko. Tokyo : Tsurushobo Publications Limited.

Hai Preso una Cotta, Charlie Brown! Milan : Milano Libri Edizione.

Buon Natale, Charlie Brown! Milan : Milano Libri Edizione.

Arriva al Cinema, Charlie Brown. Milan : Milano Libri Edizione.

Le Sentenze di Snoopy. Milan : Milano Libri Edizione.

Il Bracchetto e Charlie Brown! Milan : Milano Libri Edizione.

†Snoopy e il Suo Sopwith. Milan : Milano Libri Edizione.

Radiserne 11. Copenhagen : Gyldendal.

Søndags-Radiserne 10. Copenhagen : Gyldendal.

Radisebogen 2. Copenhagen : Gyldendal.

Radiseliv. Copenhagen : Gyldendal.

**Søren Brun Falder I Staver.* Copenhagen : Gyldendal.

Sol, sommer og Radiser. Copenhagen : Illustrationsforlaget.

Tomas Yndlings Laererinde. Copenhagen : Illustrationsforlaget.

Kaere Blyantsven! Copenhagen : Illustrationsforlaget.

Psykiatrisk Hjaelp. Copenhagen : Illustrationsforlaget.

Altså Små Brødre. Copenhagen : Illustrationsforlaget.

Altså Små Søstre. Copenhagen : Illustrationsforlaget.

1971

†*Snoopy and "It Was a Dark and Stormy Night."* New York : Holt, Rinehart and Winston.

L'Increvable Charlie Brown. New York : Holt, Rinehart and Winston.

Siempre a Flote, Charlie Brown. New York : Holt, Rinehart and Winston.

You've Come a Long Way, Charlie Brown. New York : Holt, Rinehart and Winston.

**Play It Again, Charlie Brown.* New York : World.

You're the Greatest, Charlie Brown (selected Vol. 2 from *As You Like It, Charlie Brown*). New York : Fawcett.

It's for You, Snoopy (selected Vol. 1 from *Sunday's Fun Day, Charlie Brown*). New York : Fawcett.

Have It Your Way, Charlie Brown (selected Vol. 2 fom *Sunday's Fun Day, Charlie Brown*). New York : Fawcett.

You're Not for Real, Snoopy (selected Vol. 1 from *You Need Help, Charlie Brown*). New York : Fawcett.

†*Snoopy and His Sopwith Camel.* New York : Fawcett.

***A Boy Named Charlie Brown.* New York : Fawcett.

Charlie Brown and Snoopy. London : Hodder Fawcett.

What Next, Charlie Brown. London : Hodder Fawcett.

Wonderful World of Peanuts. London : Hodder Fawcett.

You're the Greatest, Charlie Brown. London : Hodder Fawcett.

You've Done It Again, Charlie Brown. London : Hodder Fawcett.

What Were You Saying, Charlie Brown. London : Knight Books.

Snobben Flygarässet. Stockholm : Tidens Förlag.

**Snobben, Karl och Lagledartröjan.* Stockholm : Tidens Förlag.

**Kesä on Mennyt, Jaska Jokunen.* Helsinki : Sanoma Oy.

†*Ressu Ja Hänen Kaksitasonsa.* Helsinki : Sanoma Oy.

Kyllä Sina Pärjäät, Jaska Jokunen. Helsinki : Sanoma Oy.

Varo Laakapalloa, Jaska Jokunen. Helsinki : Sanoma Oy.

Ressu ja Hänen Kaksitasonsa. Helsinki : Sanoma Oy.

Yrittänyttä ei Laiteta, Jaska Jokunen. Helsinki : Sanoma Oy.

Ets Unic, Charlie Brown! Barcelona : Edicions 62.

No Perdis el Cap, Charlie Brown! Barcelona : Edicions 62.

Necessito Amics! Barcelona : Edicions 62.

L'Has Feta Bona, Charlie Brown! Barcelona : Edicions 62.

Carlitos y Snoopy San Sebastián : Buru Lan, S.A. de Ediciones.

Friskt mot, Baltus! Olso : Chr. Schibsteds Forlag.

Knøttene på Hjemmebane. Oslo : Chr. Schibsteds Forlag.

Hurra for Knøttene. Olso : Chr. Schibsteds Forlag.

Das Grosse Peanuts Buch. Götzenhain : Aar Verlag.

Au Weia, Charlie Braun! Götzenhain : Aar Verlag.

Snoopy, der Bruchpilot. Götzenhain : Aar Verlag.

Linus—Oder: Wo Bleibt der grosse Kürbis? Götzenhain : Aar Verlag.

Snoopy schreibt ein Buch. Götzenhain : Aar Verlag.

***Charlie Brown ist fast der Grösste.* Reinbek : Carlsen Verlag.

Wakkateruno Charlie Brown. Tokyo : Tsurushobo Publications Limited.

Urrekko Snoopy. Tokyo : Tsurushobo Publications Limited.

Damatteteyo Lucy. Tokyo : Tsurushobo Publications Limited.

Beale Chookan Snoopy. Tokyo : Tsurushobo Publications Limited.

Yasashii Hitone Charlie Brown. Tokyo : Tsurushobo Publications Limited.

Yamete! Lucy. Tokyo : Tsurushobo Publications Limited.

Hashire! Linus. Tokyo : Tsurushobo Publications Limited.

Kocchimuite Charlie Brown. Tokyo : Tsurushobo Publications Limited.

Soratobu Snoopy. Tokyo : Tsurushobo Publications Limited.

Sotto Oyasumi Snoopy. Tokyo : Tsurushobo Publications Limited.

**Koishiterundayo Charlie Brown.* Tokyo : Tsurushobo Publications Limited.

**Kimino Inudaze Charlie Brown.* Tokyo : Tsurushobo Publications Limited.

**Charlie Brown All-Stars.* Tokyo : Tsurushobo Publications Limited.

**Mizikai Natsudattane Charlie Brown.* Tokyo : Tsurushobo Publications Limited.

Lucy no Mooretsu Eikaiwa Gakko. Tokyo : Tsurushobo Publications Limited.

Linus no Oshaburi Eikaiwa Gakko. Tokyo : Tsurushobo Publications Limited.

Charlie, Charlie Brown. Milan : Milano Libri Edizione.

Parla, Charlie Brown. Milan : Milano Libri Edizione.

La Scuola di Linus. Milan : Milano Libri Edizione.

5500 Charlie Brown. Milan : Garzanti Editore.

Radiserne 12. Copenhagen : Gyldendal.

Søndags-Radiserne 11. Copenhagen : Gyldendal.

Radisenbogen 3. Copenhagen : Gyldendal.

**Det Er Din Hund, Søren Brun*. Copenhagen : Gyldendal.

1972

†*Snoopy's Grand Slam*. New York : Holt, Rinehart and Winston.

***The "Snoopy, Come Home" Movie Book*. New York : Holt, Rinehart and Winston.

Tu Es dans le Vent, Charlie Brown. New York : Holt, Rinehart and Winston.

Tu N'en Reviendras Pas, Charlie Brown. New York : Holt, Rinehart and Winston.

Te Vas a Desnucar, Charlie Brown. New York : Holt, Rinehart and Winston.

Eres Increíble, Charlie Brown. New York : Holt, Rinehart and Winston.

"Ha Ha, Herman," Charlie Brown. New York : Holt, Rinehart and Winston.

**You're Not Elected, Charlie Brown*. New York : World.

You're a Pal, Snoopy (selected Vol. 2 from *You Need Help, Charlie Brown*). New York : Fawcett.

What Now, Charlie Brown (selected Vol. 1 from *The Unsinkable Charlie Brown*). New York : Fawcett.

You're Something Special, Snoopy (selected Vol. 2 from *The Unsinkable Charlie Brown*). New York : Fawcett.

You've Got a Friend, Charlie Brown (selected Vol. 1 from *You'll Flip, Charlie Brown*). New York : Fawcett.

Have It Your Way, Charlie Brown. London : Hodder Fawcett.

It's for You, Snoopy. London : Hodder Fawcett.

You're Not for Real, Snoopy. London : Hodder Fawcett.

**Snobben, Karl och den Korta Sommaren*. Stockholm : Tidens Förlag.

Hyva Tavaton, Jaska Jokunen. Helsinki : Sanoma Oy.

Fes Volar L'Estel, Charlie Brown! Barcelona : Edicions 62.

†*Snoopy y el Baró Roig*. Barcelona : Edicions 62.

Torna a Casa, Snoopy. Barcelona : Edicions 62.

Fue un Corto Verano, Carlitos. San Sebastián : Buru Lan, S.A. de Ediciones.

Somos Tu Equipo, Carlitos. San Sebastián : Buru Lan, S.A. de Ediciones.

Es Navidad, Carlitos. San Sebastián : Buru Lan, S.A. de Ediciones.

Snoopy Es Tu Perro, Carlitos. San Sebastián : Buru Lan, S.A. de Ediciones.

Es la Gran Calabaza, Carlitos. San Sebastián : Buru Lan, S.A. de Ediciones.

Estás Enmorado, Carlitos. San Sebastián : Buru Lan, S.A. de Ediciones.

Snoopy, Vuelve a Casa. San Sebastián : Buru Lan, S.A. de Ediciones.

Godt Gjort, Baltus. Oslo : Chr. Schibsteds Forlag.

Knøttene i toppform. Oslo : Chr. Schibsteds Forlag.

Dein Snoopy hat Sorgen, Charlie Braun! Götzenhain : Aar Verlag.

Frohe Ferien, Charlie Braun! Götzenhain : Aar Verlag.

Liebe tut weh, Charlie Braun! Götzenhain : Aar Verlag.

Die Mannschaft braucht Dich, Charlie Brown. Götzenhain : Aar Verlag.

Snoopy: Das Zweite Grosse Peanuts Buch. Götzenhain : Aar Verlag.

Kijk, Daar Heb Je Snoopy. Utrecht/Antwerp : A. W. Bruna & Zoon.

Incasseren, Charlie Brown. Utrecht/Antwerp : A. W. Bruna & Zoon.

Hup, Charlie Brown. Utrecht/Antwerp : A. W. Bruna & Zoon.

Goeie Ouwe Snoopy. Utrecht/Antwerp : A. W. Bruna & Zoon.

Sayonara-ne Lucy. Tokyo : Tsurushobo Publications Limited.

Ouchiga kajida Snoopy. Tokyo : Tsurushobo Publications Limited.

Shitsuren shicchatta Snoopy. Tokyo : Tsurushobo Publications Limited.

Makeruna! Charlie Brown. Tokyo : Tsurushobo Publications Limited.

Senkyosendayo Snoopy. Tokyo : Tsurushobo Publications Limited.

Kekkonshitaino Lucy. Tokyo : Tsurushobo Publications Limited.

Puxa Vida, Charlie Brown. Rio de Janeiro : Artenova.

Ôi, Snoopy. Rio de Janeiro : Artenova.

É Isso Ai, Linus! Rio de Janeiro : Artenova.

Assim Não Dápé, Lucy! Rio de Janeiro : Artenova.

Assim Já é Demais, Charlie Brown. Rio de Janeiro : Artenova.

Snoopy, Volte Pra Casa! Rio de Janeiro. Artenova.

Ele é o Seu Cachorro, Charlie Brown! Rio de Janeiro : Editora de Orientação.

Feliz Natal, Charlie Brown! Rio de Janeiro : Editora de Orientação.

Foi Um Curto Verão, Charlie Brown. Rio de Janeiro : Editora de Orientação.

Você está Amando, Charlie Brown. Rio de Janeiro : Editora de Orientação.

Este é o Seu Conjunto, Charlie Brown. Rio de Janeiro : Editora de Orientação.

Una Zucca per Snoopy. Milan : Milano Libri Edizione.

Ti Saluto, Charlie Brown! Milan : Milano Libri Edizione.

Era una Notte Buia e Tempestosa. Milan : Milano Libri Edizione.

Ma che Musica, Charlie Brown. Milan : Milano Libri Edizione.

Radiserne 13. Copenhagen : Gyldendal.

Søndags-Radiserne 12. Copenhagen : Gyldendal.

Det Var en Kort Sommer, Søren Brun. Copenhagen : Gyldendal.

1973

Thompson Is in Trouble, Charlie Brown.
New York : Holt, Rinehart and Winston.

You're the Guest of Honor, Charlie Brown.
New York : Holt, Rinehart and Winston.

*There's No Time for Love, Charlie Brown.
New York : World.

*A Charlie Brown Thanksgiving. New York :
World.

Take It Easy, Charlie Brown (selected Vol. 2
from *You'll Flip, Charlie Brown*). New York :
Fawcett.

*Who Was That Dog I Saw You With, Charlie
Brown* (selected Vol. 1 from *You're You,
Charlie Brown*). New York : Fawcett.

There's No One Like You, Charlie Brown
(selected Vol. 2 from *You're You, Charlie
Brown*). New York : Fawcett.

Your Choice, Snoopy (selected Vol. 1 from
You're Something Else, Charlie Brown). New
York : Fawcett.

*Peanuts Double Volume #1 (The Wonderful
World of Peanuts and Hey, Peanuts!).* New
York : Fawcett.

***The "Snoopy, Come Home" Movie Book.*
New York : Fawcett.

Take It Easy, Charlie Brown. London :
Hodder Fawcett.

What Now, Charlie Brown. London : Hodder
Fawcett.

You're a Pal, Snoopy. London : Hodder
Fawcett.

You're Something Special, Snoopy. London :
Hodder Fawcett.

You've Got a Friend, Charlie Brown. London :
Hodder Fawcett.

†*Ressu Kirjoittaa Kirjan.* Helsinki :
Sanoma Oy.

Siinä Sitä Ollaan, Jaska Jokunen. Helsinki :
Sanoma Oy.

Necessites Ajuda, Charlie Brown!
Barcelona : Edicions 62.

Estou Na Sua, Snoopy! Rio de Janeiro :
Artenova.

É Melhor Desistir, Charlie Brown. Rio de
Janeiro : Artenova.

Muita Calma, Charlie Brown. Rio de Janeiro :
Artenova.

Duro Neles, Charlie Brown! Rio de Janeiro :
Artenova.

É Isso Ai, Lucy! Rio de Janeiro : Artenova.

Linus, Onde Tá o Grande Bruxo? Rio de
Janeiro : Artenova.

Tente Outra Vez, Charlie Brown! Rio de
Janeiro : Artenova.

Tamos Ai, Charlie Brown. Rio de Janeiro :
Artenova.

*C'est Ton Chien, Charlie Brown. Paris :
Editions M.C.L.

*Tu Es Amoureux, Charlie Brown. Paris :
Editions M.C.L.

Nytt Møte med Knøttene. Oslo : Chr.
Schibsteds Forlag.

Snoopys grosse Liebe. Götzenhain : Aar
Verlag.

Du bist süss, Charlie Brown! Götzenhain : Aar
Verlag.

Der Weltberühmte Snoopy. Götzenhain : Aar
Verlag.

Froöhliche Weihnachten, Charlie Braun!
Götzenhain : Aar Verlag.

Neue Peanuts-Geschichten. Götzenhain : Aar
Verlag.

Niente da Fare. Milan : Milano Libri Edizione.

Diavolo, Charlie Brown. Milan : Milano Libri
Edizione.

†*Snoopy, Campione di Golf.* Milan : Milano
Libri Edizione.

Snoopy Torna a Casa. Milan : Milano Libri
Edizione.

Radiserne 14. Copenhagen : Gyldendal.

Søndags-Radiserne 13. Copenhagen :
Gyldendal.

1974

Eres el Colmo, Charlie Brown. New York :
Holt, Rinehart and Winston.

Tu Es le Plus Beau, Charlie Brown. New York :
Holt, Rinehart and Winston.

Me Faire Ça a Moi, Charlie Brown. New York :
Holt, Rinehart and Winston.

Estás Perdido, Charlie Brown. New York :
Holt, Rinehart and Winston.

Win a Few, Lose a Few, Charlie Brown. New
York : Holt Rinehart and Winston.

The Snoopy Festival. New York : Holt,
Rinehart and Winston.

*It's a Mystery, Charlie Brown. New York :
World.

*It's the Easter Beagle, Charlie Brown. New
York : World.

††*The Charlie Brown Dictionary.* New York :
World.

††*Peanuts Schoolyear Datebook 1974–1975.*
San Francisco : Determined.

††*Peanuts Datebook 1975.* San Francisco :
Determined.

††*Peanuts Day by Day Book.* San Francisco :
Determined.

Try It Again, Charlie Brown (selected Vol. 2
from *You're Something Else, Charlie Brown*).
New York : Fawcett.

You've Got It Made, Charlie Brown (selected
Vol. 1 from *You've Had It Charlie Brown*).
New York : Fawcett.

Don't Give Up, Charlie Brown (selected
Vol. 2 from *You've Had It, Charlie Brown*).
New York : Fawcett.

You're So Smart, Charlie Brown (selected
Vol. 1 from *You're Out of Sight, Charlie
Brown*). New York : Fawcett.

*Peanuts Double Volume #2 (Good Grief,
Charlie Brown! and For the Love of
Peanuts!).* New York : Fawcett.

There's No-One Like You, Charlie Brown.
London : Hodder Fawcett.

Try It Again, Charlie Brown. London :
Hodder Fawcett.

*Who Was That Dog I Saw You With, Charlie
Brown.* London : Hodder Fawcett.

Your Choice, Snoopy. London : Hodder
Fawcett.

Snoopy in Springtime. London :
Brockhampton Press.

Colourful Charlie Brown. London :
Brockhampton Press.

Koeta Kestää, Jaska Jokunen. Helsinki :
Sanoma Oy.

Huipulla Tuulee, Jaska Jokunen. Helsinki : Sanoma Oy.

Les Amours de Snoopy. Paris : Hachette.

Snoopy et Compagnie. Paris : Gallimard.

Snoopy Super-Champion. Paris : Gallimard.

Snoopy S'en Va-t-en Guerre. Paris : Gallimard.

Snoopy et Ses Frères. Paris : Gallimard.

Snoopy Connaît la Musique. Paris : Gallimard.

Snoopy A des Problèmes! Paris : Gallimard.

*Je Bent Verliefd, Charlie Brown. Laren : Uitgeverij Skarabee.

*Die Hond Is Van Jou, Charlie Brown. Laren : Uitgeverij Skarabee.

Sempre Endavant, Charlie Brown. Barcelona : Edicions 62.

We Staan Achter Je, Charlie Brown. Utrecht/Antwerp : A. W. Bruna & Zoon.

Voor Mij Ben Je Een Held, Charlie Brown. Utrecht/Antwerp : A. W. Bruna & Zoon.

Zo Ben Je Non, Charlie Brown. Utrecht/Antwerp : A. W. Bruna & Zoon.

Goeie Help, Charlie Brown. Utrecht/Antwerp : A. W. Bruna & Zoon.

Udezomoo Senshu Snoopy. Tokyo : Tsurushobo Publications Limited.

Gekitsuio Snoopy. Tokyo : Tsurushobo Publications Limited.

Jy's n Doring, Charlie Brown. Durban : Republican Publications.

Si Salvi Chi Puo, Charlie Brown. Milan : Milano Libri Edizione.

E Domani, Charlie Brown. Milan : Milano Libri Edizione.

Radiserne 15. Copenhagen : Gyldendal.

Søndags Radiserne 14. Copenhagen : Gyldendal.

1975

Speak Softly, and Carry a Beagle. New York : Holt, Rinehart and Winston.

*Be My Valentine, Charlie Brown. New York : Random House.

Charlie Brown's Super Book of Things to Do and Collect. New York : Random House.

Poor Old Charlie Brown. New York : Random House.

*You're a Good Sport, Charlie Brown. New York : Random House.

What Out, Charlie Brown (selected Vol. 2 from *You're Out of Sight, Charlie Brown*). New York : Fawcett.

You're on Your Own, Snoopy (selected Vol. 1 from *"Ha Ha, Herman," Charlie Brown*). New York : Fawcett.

You Can't Win Them All, Charlie Brown (selected Vol. 2 from *"Ha Ha, Herman," Charlie Brown*). New York : Fawcett.

You've Come a Long Way, Charlie Brown. New York : Fawcett.

You've Got It Made, Snoopy. London : Hodder Fawcett.

The Peanuts Season. London : Brockhampton Press.

Snoopy on Stage. London : Brockhampton Press.

Snobbenfestivalen. Stockholm : Coeckelberghs Bokförlag.

Snobben och Gänget. Stockholm : Coeckelberghs Bokförlag.

Snobben och Karleken. Stockholm : Coeckelberghs Bokförlag.

Ressun Rakkaudet. Helsinki : Sanoma Oy.

Snoopy, O Amigo Dos Amigos! Rio de Janeiro : Artenova.

Isso É Felicidade, Charlie Brown! Rio de Janeiro : Artenova.

Les Malheurs de Charlie Brown. Paris : Hachette.

Snoopy et Son Copain Linus. Paris : Gallimard.

Snoopy: Drôles d'Oiseaux! Paris : Gallimard.

Snoopy Grand Coeur. Paris : Gallimard.

Snoopy: C'est les Vacances! Paris : Gallimard.

Snoopy et la Culture. Paris : Gallimard.

Snoopy et la Qualité de la Vie. Paris : Gallimard.

**Snoopy, Der Ausreisser. Darmstadt : Melzer, Verlag.

Snupijeve Ljubavi. Zagreb : Stvarnost Publishers.

††Il Dizionario di Peanuts. Milan : Milano Libri Edizione.